COCKTAILS

FOOD & WINE BOOKS EDITOR Anne Cain
PROJECT EDITORS Tara Stewart Hardee,
Diane Rose Keener
DESIGNER Alisha Petro
DESIGN DIRECTOR Melissa Clark
PHOTO DIRECTOR Paden Reich
COPY EDITOR Donna Baldone
PROOFREADER Jacqueline Giovanelli
INDEXER Mary Ann Laurens
FELLOW Holly Ravazzolo
PROP STYLISTS Missie Neville Crawford,
Kathleen Varner
FOOD STYLISTS Margaret Monroe Dickey,
Karen Schroeder-Rankin
Trade Edition ISBN-13: 978-0-8487-5613-0
Direct Mail Edition ISBN-13:
978-0-8487-6112-7
Library of Congress Control Number:
2018954394
First Edition 2018
Printed in the United States of America
10 9 8 7 6 5 4 3 2 1

FOOD & WINE MAGAZINE

EDITOR IN CHIEF Hunter Lewis
EXECUTIVE EDITOR Karen Shimizu
MANAGING EDITOR Caitlin Murphee Miller
EXECUTIVE WINE EDITOR Ray Isle
SENIOR FOOD EDITOR Mary-Frances Heck
CULINARY DIRECTOR Justin Chapple

We welcome your comments and
suggestions about Time Inc. Books.

Time Inc. Books
Attention: Book Editors
P.O. Box 62310
Tampa, Florida 33662-2310

Time Inc. Books products may be
purchased for business or promotional use.
For information on bulk purchases, please
contact Christi Crowley in the Special Sales
Department at (845) 895-9858.

FRONT COVER From left: Moscow Mule,
p. 101; Skyliner, p. 100; Citrus 75,
p. 33; Sazerac, p. 133

BACK COVER From left: Queen's Park
Swizzle, p. 53; Skyliner, p. 100;
Moscow Mule, p. 101

PHOTOGRAPHER Eva Kolenko
For additional photo contributors,
see p. 271.

From left: Truffled Popcorn, p. 211;
Normandie Club Spritz, p. 155;
The Doubting Duck, p. 150;
Norseman, p. 48

FOOD&WINE

COCKTAILS

More Than 150 Drinks + Appetizers and Party Menus

Welcome to *Cocktails*—featuring more than 150 recipes for classic drinks, innovative craft cocktails, and chef-created bar snacks. At FOOD & WINE, we strive to inspire and empower our wine- and food-obsessed community to eat, drink, and entertain better every day and everywhere, and we think this book will help you do just that.

A must-have handbook for any cocktail connoisseur, *Cocktails* features recipes created by today's drink tastemakers and mixologists—organized in chapters by base spirit. In addition to the cocktail recipes, you'll find tips on stocking your home bar with glassware and tools, mixology basics, a guide to essential spirits, a bar lexicon, and recipes for homemade mixers. We've also included a chapter of large-format drinks as well as nonalcoholic beverages. Because food and drinks go hand-in-hand, the Bar Food chapter contains recipes for popular snacks from the country's most notable chefs, and beginning on page 250, there are 24 party menus pairing seasonal cocktails and snacks.

Whether you're a traditionalist needing to know how to make a perfect martini or you're an adventurer wanting to explore the world of craft cocktails, this is the definitive resource for sophisticated home bartenders. Please join us in raising a glass to the perfect cocktail. Cheers!

—The Editors

From left: The Doubting
Duck, p. 150; Sonoma, p. 149

CONTENTS

Getting Started

ESSENTIAL SPIRITS

APERITIFS (WINE-BASED)

The word aperitif is often used to refer to any predinner drink, but aperitifs are also a category of beverage: light, dry, and low-proof, with characteristic bitter flavors. A century ago, mixologists began adding wine-based aperitifs to cocktails instead of simply serving them on their own before meals. Wine-based aperitifs include quinquinas (or kinas); these contain quinine, a bitter extract from cinnamon-like cinchona bark. Some well-known examples are Lillet and Dubonnet. Lillet comes in white, rosé, and red versions and is infused with citrus and subtle herb flavors. Dubonnet is a sweet blend of fortified wine, herbs, and spices.

APERITIFS (SPIRIT-BASED)

Low-proof, bitter spirit-based aperitifs like Campari have always been popular in Europe. Now they're beloved in the US thanks to mixologists' embrace of bottles like Aperol, the bitter orange Italian aperitif. Other examples of spirit-based aperitifs are Pimm's No. 1, a gin-based English aperitif with subtle spice and citrus flavors; and Cynar, which is made from 13 different herbs and plants, including artichokes.

BRANDY

Brandies are distilled from a fermented mash of fruit. French grape brandies like Armagnac and Cognac are named for the regions where they are made. Calvados is brandy made from apples (and sometimes pears) in the Normandy region of France. Applejack is an American apple brandy blended with neutral spirits. Other styles include pisco, distilled from aromatic grapes in Peru and Chile; and eau-de-vie, a specialty of the European Alps, distilled from a fermented fruit mash and bottled without aging. *(See p. 142 for more information on brandy and for brandy-based cocktails.)*

GIN

Gin is made by distilling a neutral grain spirit with botanicals such as juniper, coriander, and citrus peels. The most ubiquitous style of gin is London dry. Plymouth gin is less dry and juniper-forward, while Old Tom gin is slightly sweeter than London dry. New Western gins, such as Hendrick's, incorporate unusual botanicals like rose petals. Genever, a predecessor to gin, is a botanically rich, malted grain–based spirit. Aquavit, like gin, is made from a neutral alcohol and botanicals such as caraway, citrus peels and star anise. *(See p. 28 for more information on gin and for gin-based cocktails.)*

LIQUEURS

Among some of the oldest spirits, liqueurs are produced from a base alcohol that's distilled or macerated with a variety of ingredients, then sweetened. Sugar generally makes up to 35 percent of a liqueur's weight by volume, and up to 40 percent for crème liqueurs such as crème de menthe. Liqueurs can be herbal (Chartreuse); citrus- or fruit-based (Cointreau); floral (violet-inflected parfait amour); or nut- or seed-based (nocino, made from unripe green walnuts).

RUM

Distilled from sugarcane or its residues, rums are typically produced in tropical regions. White, a.k.a. silver or light, rum can be aged, then filtered to remove color. Amber (or gold) rum is often aged in barrels for a short time; caramel is sometimes added for color. Dark rums, made with molasses, include blackstrap rum, a rich, thick variety produced from blackstrap molasses; and Demerara rum, made on the banks of Guyana's Demerara River, with a burnt-sugar flavor. Rhum agricole and cachaça are distilled from fresh sugarcane juice. *(See p. 52 for more information on rum and for rum-based cocktails.)*

TEQUILA AND MEZCAL

Authentic tequila is made from 100 percent blue agave that is harvested by hand, slow-roasted in ovens, fermented, then distilled. Blanco (white) tequila is unaged. Reposado (rested) tequila ages up to one year in barrels. Añejo (aged) tequila must be matured between one and three years. Mezcal is known for its smoky flavor, which comes from roasting the agave in earthen pits; the finest mezcals are unaged. Mezcal is not a type of tequila—tequila is actually a type of mezcal. Mezcal refers to any alcohol made from agave, whereas tequila is made from a single type of agave—Weber's blue agave, also known as agave tequilana. *(See p. 78 for more information on tequila and mezcal and for tequila-based cocktails.)*

WHISKEY

Whiskey is distilled from a fermented mash of grains, then typically matured in oak barrels. Scotland and Japan are famous for their single malts (produced from 100 percent malted barley from one distillery). Highland Scotches are single malts of various styles from Scotland's Highland area. Most peated whisky comes from Islay in Scotland. Canada favors blended whiskies high in rye, and Irish whiskeys tend to be mellow blends. America is known for its bourbon, robust rye, and unaged, white whiskeys. There's a common misconception that bourbon must be made in Kentucky; while it's true that 85 percent of the world's bourbon is produced in Kentucky, the law only specifies that it must be made in the United States. So technically there's nothing on the books that specifically says bourbon must be from the Bluegrass State. *(See p. 116 for more information on whiskey and for whiskey-based cocktails.)*

VERMOUTH

Vermouth is an aromatic fortified wine flavored with botanicals. Dry vermouth is a staple in martinis. Sweet vermouth, which is red, is best known as whiskey's partner in a Manhattan. Italian bianco and French blanc represent another style that's slightly sweeter than dry vermouth; rosé and rosato vermouths are pink, with a spicy flavor. Cocchi Vermouth di Torino is an Italian red vermouth that's drier and more complex than other red vermouths. *(See p. 142 for more information on vermouth and for vermouth-based cocktails.)*

VODKA

Produced all over the world, vodka is traditionally distilled from fermented grain or potatoes, but nearly any fruit or vegetable can be used, from grapes to beets. Most of the flavored vodkas are created by adding ingredients to a neutral spirit; the best macerate citrus, berries, or herbs in high-proof alcohol. *(See p. 96 for more information on vodka and for vodka-based cocktails.)*

BAR LEXICON

Absinthe An herbal spirit, formerly banned in the US, flavored with botanicals such as wormwood, green anise, and fennel seeds.

Allspice Dram Also known as pimento dram; a rum-based liqueur infused with Jamaican allspice berries.

Aperol A vibrant orange-red aperitif flavored with bitter orange, rhubarb, gentian, and cinchona bark.

Applejack An American apple brandy that is blended with neutral spirits.

Barolo Chinato A Nebbiolo-based fortified wine (produced in Piedmont's Barolo zone) infused with cinchona bark ("china" in Italian) and a variety of roots, herbs, and spices, including rhubarb and cardamom.

Batavia-Arrack van Oosten A spicy and citrusy rum-like spirit made in Java from sugarcane and fermented red rice.

Bénédictine An herbal liqueur with flavors of hyssop, angelica, juniper, and myrrh. According to legend, the recipe for this liqueur was developed by a French monk in 1510.

Bigallet China-China A bitter orange French liqueur made with cinchona, gentian, and lots of other spices and herbs. It gets its rich brown color from caramel.

Bitters Concentrated tinctures of bitter and aromatic herbs, roots, and spices that add complexity to drinks. Varieties include orange, chocolate, and aromatic bitters, the best known of which is Angostura. Fee Brothers come in 17 flavors and have been made in Rochester, New York, since Prohibition. Peychaud's bitters have flavors of anise and cherry.

Bonal Gentiane-Quina A slightly bitter French aperitif wine infused with gentian root and cinchona bark, which is the source of quinine.

Bonded A term used for a single-distillery–produced liquor (such as whiskey or apple brandy) that's distilled during a single season, aged at least four years, bottled at 100 proof and stored in a "bonded" warehouse under US government supervision.

Branca Menta A spin-off of the bitter Italian digestif Fernet-Branca with a pronounced peppermint and menthol flavor.

Campari A potent, bright red aperitif with a bitter orange flavor. It's made from a secret blend of fruit, herbs, and spices.

Cardamaro A Moscato-wine–based amaro infused with cardoon, an artichoke-like plant with a nutty flavor; and blessed thistle, a bitter botanical.

Carpano Antica Formula A rich and complex sweet red vermouth with notes of vanilla.

Chartreuse An intense herbal French liqueur made from more than 100 botanicals; green Chartreuse is more potent than the honey-sweetened yellow one.

Cocchi Americano A white-wine–based aperitif infused with cinchona bark, citrus peels, and herbs such as gentian. The rosa variety is more bitter and aromatic than the white.

Cocchi Vermouth Di Torino A slightly bitter, Moscato-based red vermouth with hints of citrus, rhubarb, and cocoa.

Cognac Cognac is divided into categories based on aging time: VS (Very Special) Cognacs are aged at least two years. VSOP (Very Superior Old Pale) must be aged at least four years. XO (Extra Old) are aged for at least ten years.

Cointreau A French triple sec made with sun-dried sweet and bitter orange peels.

Combier Pamplemousse Rose A pale pink French liqueur made by infusing ripe red grapefruit in a neutral alcohol.

Crème de Cacao A cacao-flavored liqueur that's less sweet than chocolate liqueur. It can be dark (brown) or white (colorless).

Curaçao A general term for orange-flavored liqueurs historically produced in the French West Indies. Blue curaçao is the same orange-flavored liqueur that has been dyed a vivid blue.

Cynar A pleasantly bitter aperitif made from 13 herbs and plants, including artichokes.

Drambuie A whisky-based Scottish liqueur flavored with honey, herbs, and spices.

Fernet-Branca A potent, bitter-flavored Italian digestif that's made from 27 herbs.

Génépy des Alpes A pungent herbal liqueur made from génépy, a rare Alpine plant also used in Chartreuse.

Gum Syrup A simple syrup that's been thickened with gum arabic, made from the sap of acacia trees.

Herbsaint An anise-flavored absinthe substitute produced in New Orleans.

Licor 43 A citrus-and-vanilla–flavored Spanish liqueur made from a combination of 43 aromatic herbs and spices.

Lillet A wine-based aperitif flavored with orange peel and quinine. The rouge variety is sweeter than the blanc. The rosé (a blend of the red and white) has a slightly fruity flavor.

Maraschino Liqueur A colorless Italian liqueur. The best brands are distilled from sour marasca cherries and their pits, and then aged and sweetened with sugar.

Orgeat A sweet syrup made from almonds or almond extract and rose or orange flower water.

Overproof A term for any spirit (such as bourbon, rum, or Cognac) that contains more than 50 percent alcohol (and so is over 100 proof).

Pastis A licorice-flavored French spirit that turns cloudy when mixed with water. It's similar to absinthe but sweeter, lower in alcohol, and made without wormwood.

Pimm's No. 1 A gin-based English aperitif flavored with spices and citrus. It's often served with ginger beer, 7 Up, or lemonade.

Port A fortified wine from the Douro region of Portugal. The styles include fruity, young ruby port; richer, nuttier tawny port; dry or sweet white port made from white grapes; and thick-textured, oak-aged, late-bottled vintage port (LBV).

Punt E Mes A spicy, orange-accented Italian sweet vermouth fortified with bitters.

Salers A French gentian root–based aperitif. It has a pronounced bitterness that's balanced by sweetness from white wine and botanicals.

Sherry A fortified wine from Spain's Jerez region. Varieties include dry styles like fino and manzanilla; nuttier, richer styles like amontillado and oloroso; and viscous, sweet Pedro Ximénez (PX), Moscatel, and cream sherry. East India sherry falls between an oloroso and a PX in style.

Shochu A Japanese low-proof spirit distilled from a variety of ingredients, such as rice, barley, sweet potatoes, buckwheat, carrots, or brown sugar.

St-Germain A French liqueur created by blending macerated elderflower blossoms with eau-de-vie. It has hints of pear, peach, and grapefruit zest.

Suze A bittersweet, aromatic, yellow aperitif made from gentian root with hints of vanilla, candied orange, and spice.

Tremontis Mirto A bittersweet liqueur from Sardinia that's made from myrtle berries.

Triple Sec An orange-flavored liqueur that is similar to curaçao but not as sweet.

Velvet Falernum A low-alcohol, sugarcane-based liqueur from Barbados flavored with clove, almond, and lime.

Verjus The tart, pressed, unfermented juice of unripe grapes—either white, red, or a mix of red and white.

Zirbenz Stone Pine Liqueur A slightly sweet liqueur made from the fruit of the arolla stone pine in Austria. It has a reddish hue and a pine aroma and flavor.

Zucca A bittersweet, slightly smoky aperitif made from rhubarb and flavored with cardamom, citrus, and vanilla.

Zwack An intense, citrus-flavored Hungarian herbal liqueur made from a blend of more than 40 herbs and spices.

GLASSWARE

Glasses are critical to a good cocktail. They don't have to be fancy or expensive, but they should be appropriate for the drinks you are making. The shape of the glass will affect both the flavor and aroma of the drink, and smaller glasses tend to be better than large. A standard cocktail served in a large glass may come to room temperature before the drink is finished.

1 · Martini
A stemmed glass with a cone-shaped bowl for cocktails served straight up (mixed with ice and then strained).

2 · Rocks
A short, widemouthed glass for spirits served neat (without ice) and cocktails poured over ice. Single rocks glasses hold 6 to 8 ounces; double rocks glasses hold 12 to 14 ounces.

3 · Collins
A very tall, narrow glass often used for drinks that are served on ice and topped with soda.

4 · Wineglass
A tall, slightly rounded, stemmed glass for wine-based cocktails. White wineglasses are a fine substitute for highball glasses and are also a good choice for frozen drinks. Balloon-shaped red wineglasses are ideal for fruity cocktails as well as punches.

5 · Highball
A tall, narrow glass for cocktails that are served with ice and topped with sparkling beverages such as club soda, tonic water, or ginger beer.

6 · Coupe

A shallow, widemouthed, stemmed glass primarily for small (short) and potent cocktails that are served straight up. Although the coupe was originally designed to hold Champagne, its shape is more decorative than functional. Most coupes have a capacity of 4 to 8 ounces.

7 · Pilsner

A tall, flared glass designed for beer. It's also good for oversized cocktails on ice, drinks with multiple garnishes, or as a substitute for a tiki mug.

8 · Heatproof Glass or Mug

A durable ceramic or glass cup with a handle. Perfect for coffee spiked with whiskey or other spirits as well as toddies and other hot drinks.

9 · Flute

A tall, slender, usually stemmed glass; its narrow shape helps keep Champagne or sparkling wine cocktails effervescent.

10 · Julep Cup

A short metal cup designed to keep juleps (minty, crushed-ice cocktails) cold. Julep cups are traditionally silver but these days can be found in copper or stainless steel.

11 · Fizz

A narrow glass for soda-topped drinks without ice. Also called a juice glass or Delmonico glass.

12 · Tiki Mug

A tall sculptural mug, usually without a handle, that's decorated with a Polynesian-style or tropical motif.

13 · Snifter (not pictured)

A wide-bowled glass for spirits served neat or potent cocktails. It's designed to focus on the aromatics of the drink and get them right to the nose. This type of glass is often used for brandy and cognac.

BAR TOOLS

1 · Hawthorne Strainer
The best all-purpose strainer.
A semicircular spring ensures
a spill-proof fit on a shaker.
Look for a tightly coiled spring,
which keeps muddled fruit
and herbs out of drinks.

2 · Jigger
A two-sided stainless steel
measuring instrument for
precise mixing. Look for double-
sided ones with ½- and ¾-ounce
measures and 1- and 2-ounce
cups. A shot glass with measures
works, too.

3 · Muddler
A sturdy tool that's used to
crush herbs, sugar cubes,
and fresh fruit; it's traditionally
made of wood.

4 · Microplane
A fine-toothed metal grater
for shaving citrus zest, ginger,
and hard spices like cinnamon
sticks and nutmeg.

5 · Julep Strainer
The preferred device for
straining cocktails from a mixing
glass because it fits securely.
Fine holes keep ice
out of the drink.

6 · Channel Knife
A small, spoon-shaped knife
with a metal tooth. Creates
long, thin spiral-cut twists from
citrus-fruit peels.

7 · Citrus Juicer
A metal or ceramic citrus press
that allows you to squeeze
lemons, limes, and oranges
à la minute.

8 · Y Peeler
A wide peeler that's great for
making large and small citrus-
fruit twists.

9 · Fine Strainer
A fine-mesh strainer held over a glass before the cocktail is poured in (see Fine-Straining Drinks, p. 20). It keeps bits of muddled herbs, fruit, and crushed ice out of drinks.

10 · Waiter's Corkscrew
A pocketknife-like tool with an attached bottle opener. Bartenders prefer it to bulkier, more complicated corkscrews.

11 · Boston Shaker
The bartender's choice; consists of a mixing glass, usually a pint glass, with a metal canister that covers the glass to create a seal. Shake drinks with the metal half pointing away from you. Alternatively, replace the mixing glass with a small shaking tin.

12 · Ice Pick
A sharp metal tool with a sturdy handle used to break off chunks from a larger block of ice.

13 · Atomizer
A small spray bottle used to disperse tiny quantities of aromatic liquid evenly over the surface of an empty glass or on top of a cocktail.

14 · Cobbler Shaker
A shaker with a metal cup for mixing drinks with ice, a built-in strainer, and a fitted top.

15 · Bar Spoon
A long-handled metal spoon that mixes cocktails without creating air bubbles. Some include a relish fork for garnishes.

MIXOLOGY BASICS

RIMMING A GLASS

Spread kosher salt, sugar, or another powdered ingredient on a small plate. Moisten half or all of the outer rim of a glass with a citrus-fruit wedge, water, or syrup; roll the rim on the plate until it is lightly coated, then tap to release any excess.

MAKING A TWIST

A small strip of citrus zest adds concentrated citrus flavor from the peel's essential oils.

Standard Twist Use a sharp paring knife or peeler to cut a thin, oval disk of the peel, avoiding the pith. Grasp the twist, skin side down, and pinch it over the drink. Then discard the twist, set it on the rim, or drop it into the drink.

Spiral-Cut Twist Working over the drink, use a channel knife to cut a long, narrow piece of peel with some pith intact. Wrap the twist around a straw; tighten at both ends to create a curlicue.

FLAMING A TWIST

Flaming a citrus twist caramelizes its essential oils. Grasp a citrus twist, skin side down, 4 inches over the drink. Hold a lit match an inch away from the twist—don't let the flame touch the peel—then pinch the twist so the citrus oils fall through the flame and into the drink.

FINE-STRAINING

Drinks made with muddled fruit or herbs are often double-strained to remove tiny particles so that the cocktail is crystal clear. First, set a fine strainer over a serving glass. Prepare the drink in a shaker or pint glass. Then set a Hawthorne or julep strainer on top, then pour the drink through both strainers into the serving glass.

SMACKING HERBS

To accentuate the aroma of fresh herbs used for garnish, clap them between your hands over the glass to release the essential oils into the drink.

STIRRING DRINKS

To mix drinks like a pro, stir gently and quietly for 20 seconds without rattling the ice.

PERFECTING ICE

The right ice is essential to preparing a balanced and attractive drink.

To make big blocks of ice, pour water into a large, shallow plastic container and freeze. To unmold, first warm the bottom of the container in hot water.

To make crushed ice, cover the ice cubes in a clean kitchen towel and pound them with a wooden mallet or rolling pin.

To make cracked ice, hold an ice cube in your hand; tap it with the back of a bar spoon so it breaks into pieces.

To make clear cubes, fill ice cube trays with hot filtered water.

To make perfectly square ice cubes, use flexible silicone Perfect Cube ice trays, available at surlatable.com or amazon.com.

Rimming a Glass

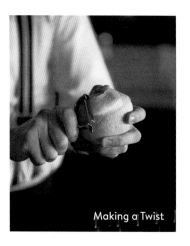

Making a Twist

Fine-Straining a Drink

Stirring a Drink

Homemade Grenadine

HOMEMADE MIXERS

Simple Syrup
MAKES ABOUT 12 OUNCES

In a small saucepan, combine 8 ounces water and 1 cup sugar and bring to a boil. Simmer over moderate heat, stirring frequently, until the sugar is dissolved, about 3 minutes. Let cool, then transfer the syrup to a bottle or jar and refrigerate for up to 1 month.

Easiest Simple Syrup
MAKES ABOUT 12 OUNCES

In a heatproof bottle or jar with a tight-fitting lid, combine 8 ounces hot water with 1 cup superfine sugar and shake until the sugar is dissolved. Let cool, then refrigerate the syrup for up to 1 month.

Rich Simple Syrup
MAKES ABOUT 8 OUNCES

In a small saucepan, combine 4 ounces water and 1 cup Demerara or other raw sugar and bring to a boil. Simmer over moderate heat, stirring, until the sugar is dissolved, about 3 minutes. Let cool, then transfer the syrup to a bottle or jar and refrigerate for up to 1 month.

Vanilla Simple Syrup
MAKES ABOUT 12 OUNCES

In a small saucepan, combine 8 ounces water, 1 cup sugar, and ½ split vanilla bean and bring to a boil. Simmer over moderate heat, stirring, until sugar dissolves, about 3 minutes. Let cool, then strain syrup into a bottle or tightly covered glass jar; refrigerate for up to 1 month.

Honey Syrup
MAKES ABOUT 6 OUNCES

In a microwavable bottle or jar, heat 4 ounces honey in a microwave for about 30 seconds at high power. Add 4 ounces warm water, cover tightly, and shake until the honey is dissolved. (Alternatively, in a small saucepan, stir 4 ounces honey and 4 ounces water over moderate heat until the honey is dissolved.) Let cool, then refrigerate the syrup for up to 1 month.

Fennel Syrup
MAKES ABOUT 6 OUNCES

In a saucepan, boil 4 ounces water. Remove from heat, add ½ cup cubed fennel (½-inch pieces cut from ½ of a small bulb), and let steep for 6 minutes. Remove and discard the fennel. Add ½ cup sugar to the saucepan and bring to a boil, stirring just until dissolved. Remove from heat, let cool, and transfer syrup to a jar. Refrigerate the syrup for up to 2 weeks.

Raspberry Syrup
MAKES ABOUT 8 OUNCES

In a medium saucepan, combine 4 ounces water, ¾ cup superfine sugar, and 1½ cups raspberries. Cook over low heat for 15 minutes, smashing the raspberries. Remove from heat and let stand for 30 minutes. Strain syrup into a jar; cover and refrigerate the syrup for up to 4 days.

Ginger Syrup
MAKES ABOUT 5 OUNCES

In a small saucepan, combine ½ cup sugar and 4 ounces water. Simmer over moderate heat, stirring until sugar dissolves. Add ⅓ cup (1½ ounces) minced fresh ginger and simmer over very low heat for 30 minutes, stirring occasionally. Let cool, then pour syrup through a fine strainer into a jar. Refrigerate for up to 2 weeks.

Spicy Ginger Syrup
MAKES ABOUT 3 OUNCES

In a jar, combine 2 ounces fresh ginger juice (from two 3-inch pieces) and ¼ cup sugar. Cover and shake until the sugar dissolves. Refrigerate for up to 2 weeks.

Cinnamon Syrup
MAKES ABOUT 24 OUNCES

In a medium saucepan, combine 16 ounces water, 2 cups sugar, and 6 medium cinnamon sticks. Stir over moderate heat until sugar is dissolved, then simmer (do not boil) for 10 minutes. Let cool. Remove the cinnamon sticks and pour syrup into a jar. Refrigerate for up to 2 weeks.

Homemade Grenadine
MAKES ABOUT 12 OUNCES

In a bottle or jar with a tight-fitting lid, shake 8 ounces unsweetened pomegranate juice and 1 cup sugar until sugar is dissolved. If desired, add ⅛ teaspoon orange flower water. Refrigerate for up to 2 weeks.

Gin & Tonic, p. 29

Gin

Gin

For a spirit to be called gin, it must be flavored with juniper berries. Beyond that, gin is not very closely regulated. It's usually made with a neutral grain distillate such as vodka and botanicals that often include spices, citrus, and herbs. Styles of gin vary widely depending on the mix of botanicals that are used and the amount of sugar added.

TYPES OF GIN

London Dry The most common and versatile style of gin, this classic is clean and unsweetened and always has a dominant juniper flavor.

Plymouth Less dry and juniper-forward than London dry, this gin is produced only in Plymouth, England. It's fuller-bodied than London dry gin and has a more earthy botanical mix.

Old Tom This gin is slightly sweeter than London dry and has a touch of malt flavor.

Sloe Gin A bittersweet red liqueur with a nutty finish made by infusing a neutral grain spirit or gin with sloe berries and sugar. It's typically used in a drink called a sloe gin fizz.

Genever The predecessor to gin, genever is a botanically rich, malted grain–based spirit with a malty, hearty, whiskey-like quality. It can be made only in Holland or Belgium.

Modern These new gins with less juniper flavor and more focus on citrus, herbs, and spices are popular in craft cocktails. The taste is somewhere between flavored vodka and London dry.

Aquavit This neutral spirit distilled from grain or potato has much in common with gin, but rather than juniper as its main element, it's flavor comes from caraway and a blend of herbs and spices.

GIN GUIDELINES

While vodka simply disappears into a drink, gin has a more assertive flavor and is a little trickier to blend. When a combination is successful, though, it attains a level of complexity that's impossible with vodka.

Try aromatic mixers. The botanicals in gin make it a natural match for aromatized wines (vermouth, Lillet), bitter spirits (Campari), and concentrated bitters (Angostura, Peychaud's or orange bitters).

Use fresh citrus juices. Most gins are flavored with orange and lemon peel; for that reason, they work well in cocktails that contain sweetened citrus juice.

Chill thoroughly. The best way to compare brands of gin is to taste them at room temperature, but mixed gin drinks should be icy cold. Use plenty of ice and chilled club soda or tonic (keep bottles in the refrigerator) and, if using a shaker, shake it until it is almost too cold to hold.

GIN & TONIC

1½ oz. gin, preferably Plymouth

4 oz. chilled tonic water, preferably Fentimans

Ice

1 or 2 lime wedges, for garnish

PHOTO ON P. 26

Once a mainstay of country clubs, the gin and tonic has become a popular drink at US tapas restaurants, a trend that started in Spain.

In a chilled highball glass, combine gin and tonic water; fill glass with ice and stir well. Garnish with lime wedges. —*Todd Thrasher*

How to Make the Perfect Gin & Tonic

"In Spain, gin-tonic is not just a cocktail, it is an obsession," says famed Spanish chef José Andrés. Here's everything you need to know to nail this iconic drink at home:

Garnish with fresh herbs and aromatics. In Spain, lemon verbena, rosemary or lavender, lemon peel, juniper berries, edible flowers, and even whole spices are used to enhance the gin's botanicals.

Stock up. Spanish bars carry as many as 50 different gins. Our choice: Plymouth or a London dry style. José's two favorites: Rives Special Premium Tridestilada from Andalusia and Xoriguer Gin de Mahón from Menorca.

Amplify the aroma of the gin and the garnishes with a large wineglass or goblet.

Use big ice cubes to keep your gin-tonic chilled without watering it down.

Look for tonic made with cane sugar or agave (not high-fructose syrup), such as Q, Fever-Tree, or Fentimans, for a balanced mix of sweetness cut with quinine bitterness.

NEGRONI

——— MAKES 1 DRINK ———

1 oz. gin, preferably London dry

1 oz. Campari

1 oz. sweet vermouth

Ice

1 orange twist, for garnish

This classic bittersweet cocktail, often served as a before-meal drink, probably got its name from Camillo Negroni, a Florentine aristocrat who asked a bartender to make his Americano (sweet vermouth, Campari, and club soda) with gin instead of soda. The sweet vermouth offsets some of the bitterness of the Campari.

In a mixing glass, combine gin, Campari and vermouth; fill with ice and stir well. Strain into a chilled coupe; pinch orange twist over drink and add to glass. Alternatively, strain into a chilled, ice-filled rocks glass and garnish.

TINGLING NEGRONI

——— MAKES 1 DRINK ———

1 oz. London dry gin

1 oz. Aperol

½ oz. Cynar (bitter, artichoke-flavored aperitif)

½ oz. Zirbenz Stone Pine Liqueur of the Alps

Ice

4 drops of Sichuan Peppercorn Oil

1 rosemary sprig, for garnish

"I wanted to do a Negroni unlike any other," says New York City bartender Sam Anderson. In place of the traditional sweet vermouth, he stirs in pine fruit liqueur (pine fruit matures into a pinecone). Anderson then adds a few drops of numbing Sichuan peppercorn oil "for a whiff of strange."

In a mixing glass, combine gin, Aperol, Cynar and pine liqueur; fill with ice and stir well. Strain into a chilled, ice-filled rocks glass. Dot peppercorn oil over surface of drink and garnish with rosemary sprig. —*Sam Anderson*

SICHUAN PEPPERCORN OIL
In a spice grinder, coarsely grind 2 teaspoons Sichuan peppercorns. In a small saucepan, combine ground peppercorns with ¼ cup peanut oil and cook over moderate heat, swirling occasionally, until peppercorns darken, about 1 minute. Let cool, then pour into a jar. Refrigerate oil for up to 3 months. Bring to room temperature and stir before using. Makes ¼ cup.

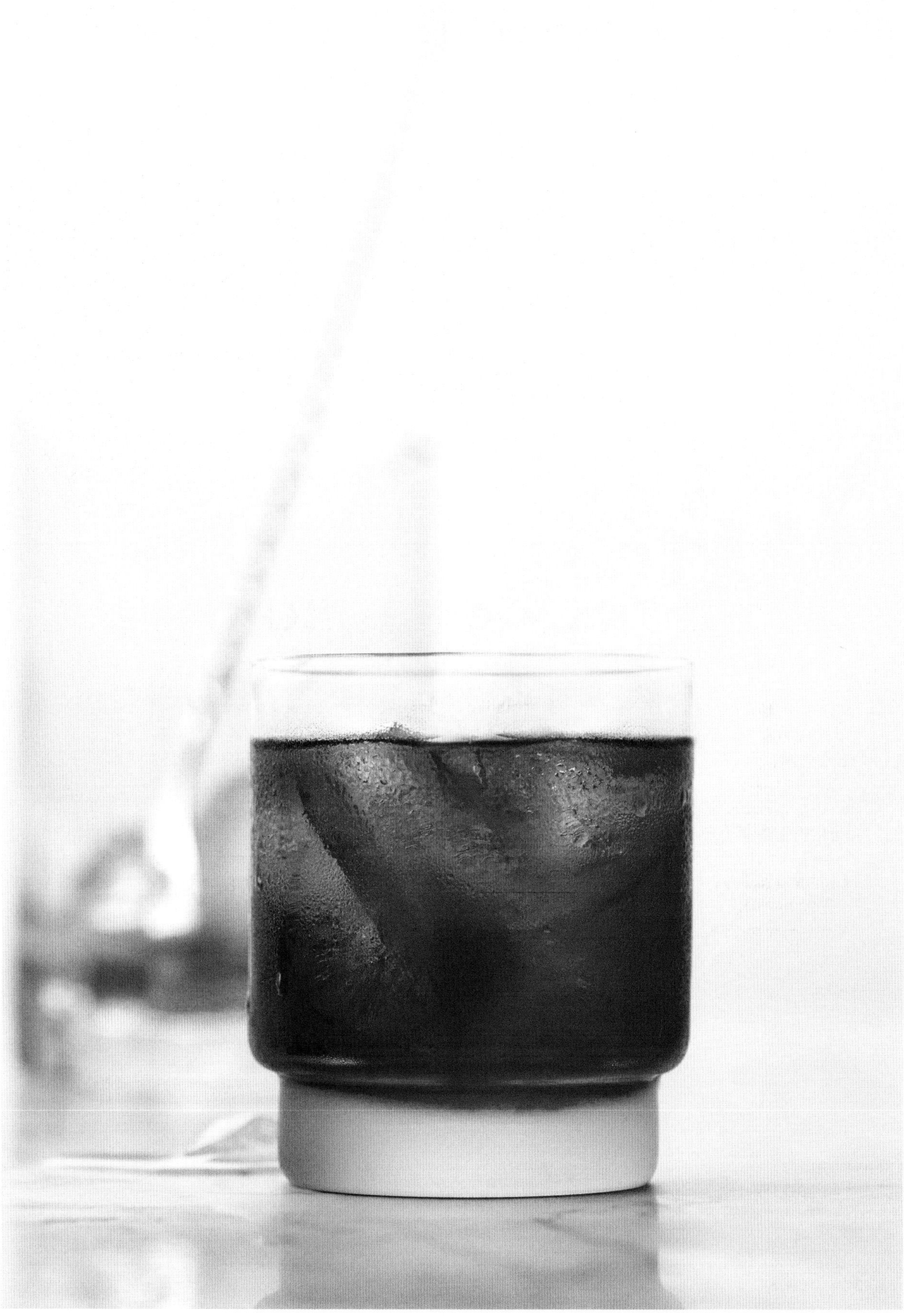

MARTINI

— MAKE 1 DRINKS —

- 3 oz. gin
- 1 oz. dry vermouth
- 2 dashes of orange bitters
- Ice
- 1 green olive or 1 lemon twist, for garnish

The original martini, allegedly invented in the US in the 1860s, was made with sweet vermouth. One of the first recipes for a dry martini, made with dry vermouth, appeared in Frank P. Newman's 1904 *American Bar*. Despite James Bond's preference, most bartenders will insist that this classic be stirred, not shaken with ice, to prevent it from becoming watered down.

In a mixing glass, combine gin, vermouth, and bitters. Fill glass with ice and stir well. Strain into a chilled martini glass or coupe and garnish with olive or lemon twist.

CLASSIC

TOM COLLINS

— MAKES 1 DRINK —

- 1½ oz. London dry gin
- ¾ oz. fresh lemon juice
- ¾ oz. Simple Syrup (p. 23)
- Ice
- 2 oz. chilled club soda
- 1 lemon twist, for garnish

Cocktail historians credit this classic summer gin drink to John Collins, a waiter at Limmer's Old House in 1800s London. The "Tom" part came along when bartenders began making it with Old Tom gin, which is slightly sweet. Although the name stuck, London dry gin now forms the base of the modern Tom Collins.

In a chilled collins glass, combine gin, lemon juice, and Simple Syrup. Fill glass with ice and stir well. Stir in club soda and garnish with lemon twist. —*Marcos Tello*

FRENCH 75

MAKES 1 DRINK

1 oz. gin

½ oz. fresh lemon juice

½ oz. Simple Syrup (p. 23)

Ice

4 oz. chilled brut Champagne

Many believe this drink was devised by American soldiers in France during World War I who were hankering for a Tom Collins. They had gin and lemons but no soda, so they used what was at hand: Champagne. The result was named for the French-made 75-millimeter guns.

In a cocktail shaker, combine gin, lemon juice, and Simple Syrup. Fill shaker with ice and shake well. Strain into a chilled flute and top with Champagne.

Note

For another version of the classic French 75, see the recipe for a Clementine 75 (p. 145).

CITRUS 75

MAKES 1 DRINK

½ clementine

1½ oz. gin

¾ oz. fresh lemon juice

½ oz. limoncello

½ oz. honey syrup (½ Tbsp. honey mixed with ½ Tbsp. warm water)

Ice

1 oz. chilled brut Champagne

1 lemon twist and 1 orange wheel, for garnish

Kathy Casey of Kathy Casey Liquid Kitchen likes making her own limoncello, the sweet Italian lemon liqueur, for this tangy version of a French 75. Pallini limoncello, which is widely available, also works well here.

In a cocktail shaker, muddle clementine. Add gin, lemon juice, limoncello, honey syrup, and ice; shake well. Strain into a chilled coupe, top with Champagne and garnish with lemon twist and orange wheel. *—Kathy Casey*

Aviation

BRONX

1½ oz. London dry gin

1 oz. fresh orange juice

½ oz. sweet vermouth

½ oz. dry vermouth

Ice

The Bronx became a popular drink around 1910, possibly because it was one of the first to contain orange juice. In 1934, *Burke's Complete Cocktail and Drinking Recipes* ranked it as the third most famous cocktail in the world, after the martini and the Manhattan.

In a cocktail shaker, combine gin, orange juice, and both vermouths. Fill shaker with ice and shake well. Strain into a chilled coupe.

AVIATION

2 oz. gin

¾ oz. fresh lemon juice

⅜ oz. maraschino liqueur

⅜ oz. crème de violette (violet liqueur)

Ice

1 sour cherry, preferably marasca, for garnish (optional)

The original 1916 Aviation included crème de violette, a violet-flavored liqueur that tinted the drink a pale sky blue (hence the cocktail's name, some say). Later, the liqueur became impossible to find in the US, and a version without it became the standard. Today, the liqueur is available again: At least three new brands have launched within the last decade.

In a cocktail shaker, combine gin, lemon juice, maraschino liqueur, and violet liqueur. Fill shaker with ice and shake well. Strain into a chilled coupe and garnish with the cherry.

GIN FIZZ

2 oz. London dry gin

¾ oz. fresh lime juice

¾ oz. Simple Syrup (p. 23)

Ice

1½ oz. club soda

1 maraschino cherry,
for garnish

The gin fizz, a sour-based cocktail with club soda, was all the rage in the US until the mid-20th century. This eggless version is the original.

In a cocktail shaker, combine gin, lime juice, and Simple Syrup. Fill shaker with ice and shake well. Strain into a chilled, ice-filled highball glass, stir in club soda, and garnish the drink with a maraschino cherry.

Gin Fizz Upgrades

Spritzy and refreshing, a gin fizz is simply made with gin, lemon or lime juice, simple syrup, and club soda (plus an optional egg white if you want to make it a silver fizz). And while the original, sweet-tart cocktail is delicious, it can be tweaked and tinkered with to fit your tastes. Here are four ways to reinvent the gin fizz:

Add some herbs. Swap out the sugar for an aromatic rosemary simple syrup. Garnished with a sprig of fresh rosemary, it's the perfect holiday cocktail.

Infuse it with tea. Infuse gin with jasmine tea for a beautifully floral take on the citrusy cocktail.

Give it some color. Concord grapes and port give the frothy cocktail a vibrant purple color and deep, fruity flavor.

Make it tropical. Muddled lychees and lemongrass syrup transform the cocktail into a sweet and exotic drink.

RAMOS GIN FIZZ

MAKES 1 DRINK

¾ oz. fresh lemon juice

1 large egg white

2 oz. gin, preferably Plymouth

1½ oz. chilled heavy cream

1 oz. Simple Syrup (p. 23)

8 drops of orange flower water

Ice

1½ oz. chilled club soda

1 orange twist, for garnish

There are several classic recipes for the Ramos Gin Fizz. Bartender Rhiannon Enlil prefers a "creamier, boozier, and more floral" one to the lighter version published in the 1928 *New Orleans Item-Tribune* by bartender Henry Charles Ramos. Enlil agrees with Ramos, however, that you must "shake and shake and shake until there is not a bubble left but the drink is smooth and snowy white and the consistency of good rich milk."

In a cocktail shaker, combine lemon juice and egg white and shake well. Add gin, heavy cream, Simple Syrup, orange flower water, and ice and shake again. Pour club soda into a chilled collins glass, then slowly strain the drink into glass. Garnish with orange twist and serve with a straw. —*Rhiannon Enlil*

CLASSIC

CORPSE REVIVER NO. 2

MAKES 1 DRINK

¼ oz. absinthe

1 oz. gin

1 oz. Cointreau or other triple sec

1 oz. Lillet blanc

1 oz. fresh lemon juice

Ice

According to Harry Craddock's seminal *Savoy Cocktail Book* of 1930, this tart cocktail should be consumed as a pick-me-up. "But four of these taken in swift succession will unrevive the corpse again," he warns.

Rinse a chilled martini glass with absinthe; pour out the excess. In a cocktail shaker, combine gin, Cointreau, Lillet, and lemon juice. Fill shaker with ice, shake well, and strain into prepared martini glass.

BEE'S KNEES

—— MAKES 1 DRINK ——

2 oz. gin

¾ oz. fresh lemon juice

¾ oz. honey syrup
(1 Tbsp. honey mixed with
½ Tbsp. warm water)

Ice

This honey-sweetened Prohibition-era cocktail makes New York City bartender Lynnette Marrero think of spring: "It's simple, clean, and refreshing–like a winter toddy that's gotten a spring makeover," she says.

In a cocktail shaker, combine gin, lemon juice, and honey syrup. Fill with ice and shake well. Strain into a chilled coupe.
—*Lynnette Marrero*

LAVENDER GIN COCKTAIL

—— MAKES 1 DRINK ——

2 Tbsp. dried lavender buds

1 cup boiling water

2 oz. tonic water, preferably Fever-Tree

1 oz. London dry gin

1 oz. fresh lime juice, plus 1 lime wedge for garnish

½ oz. agave syrup

Ice

1 lavender sprig, for garnish

This spritzy, floral cocktail from La Granja in Ibiza, Spain, will make anyone a gin drinker. The lavender plays perfectly with a botanical-forward gin, and a touch of lime juice and agave round out the whole thing. This is definitely the new drink of summer.

1 Place dried lavender buds in a small heatproof bowl. Pour boiling water over the top and let steep for 30 minutes. Strain lavender infusion through a fine sieve set over a small bowl; discard the solids. Cover and refrigerate until cold.

2 In a cocktail shaker, combine tonic water, gin, lime juice, agave, and ½ ounce of lavender infusion; fill with ice and shake well. Strain into an ice-filled rocks glass or cup and garnish with lime wedge and lavender sprig. Use the remaining lavender infusion to make more cocktails. —*F&W*

Make Ahead
The lavender infusion can be refrigerated for up to 1 week.

Lavender Gin Cocktail

SOUTHSIDE

— MAKES 1 DRINK —

10 mint leaves, plus 2 mint
   sprigs for garnish

2 oz. gin

¾ oz. fresh lemon juice

½ oz. Rich Simple Syrup (p. 23)

¼ oz. fresh lime juice

   Ice

According to one story, this cocktail was the preferred beverage of Al Capone, whose gang dominated Chicago's South Side. The gin imported by Capone's rivals on the North Side of Chicago was smooth, and usually consumed with ginger ale, but the gin run by Capone's gang had a rougher edge to it, and required more sweeteners to make it palatable–and the Southside cocktail was born. The cocktail is also said to have originated at the Southside Sportsmen's Club on Long Island.

In a cocktail shaker, muddle mint leaves. Add gin, lemon juice, Rich Simple Syrup, lime juice, and ice and shake well. Fine-strain (p.20) into a chilled coupe. Smack (p.20) the mint sprigs over the drink, then add them to the glass as garnish.
—*Daniel Shoemaker*

SINGAPORE SLING

— MAKES 1 DRINK —

1½ oz. gin, preferably Plymouth

1½ oz. chilled pineapple juice

1 oz. Sling Business

½ oz. fresh lime juice

   Dash of Angostura bitters

   Ice

1 brandied cherry skewered
   on a pick with 1 pineapple
   wedge, for garnish

"The Singapore Sling is one of my favorite tropical cocktails," says New York City mixologist Julie Reiner. Most drink histories credit the recipe to a bartender named Ngiam Tong Boon, who's said to have mixed the first Sling around 1915 at the Long Bar inside Singapore's Raffles Hotel.

In a cocktail shaker combine gin, pineapple juice, Sling Business, lime juice, and bitters. Fill with ice and shake well. Strain into a chilled, ice-filled coupe and garnish with the cherry and pineapple wedge. —*Julie Reiner*

SLING BUSINESS

In a jar, combine ¼ ounce each of Heering cherry liqueur, Bénédictine (brandy-based herbal liqueur), grenadine (preferably homemade, p.23), and Cointreau or other triple sec. Makes 1 ounce.

ROSEMARY SALTY DOG

MAKES 1 DRINK

1 grapefruit wedge

Kosher salt

One 1-inch piece of rosemary sprig, plus 1 sprig for garnish

½ teaspoon sugar

2 oz. fresh red grapefruit juice

1½ oz. gin

Ice

North Carolina chef Ashley Christensen adds muddled fresh rosemary to her version of the gin–and–grapefruit juice classic cocktail.

Moisten the outer rim of a chilled martini glass with grapefruit wedge and coat lightly with salt. In a cocktail shaker, muddle 1-inch rosemary sprig with sugar. Add grapefruit juice, gin, and ice and shake vigorously. Strain into prepared martini glass and garnish with remaining rosemary sprig. —*Ashley Christensen*

WHEN THE BRITISH CAME TO SPAIN

MAKES 1 DRINK

1½ oz. Plymouth gin

1 oz. fino sherry

¾ tsp. fresh lemon juice

¾ tsp. grenadine, preferably homemade (p. 23)

¾ tsp. curaçao

¾ tsp. French dry vermouth, such as Dolin

Ice

"I'm a big fan of dry martinis," says Ezra Star of Drink in Boston. "I wanted a martini-like drink that was salty and briny." She gives her drink extra flavor with sherry and a rosy tinge with grenadine.

In a mixing glass, combine all ingredients except ice. Fill glass with ice and stir well. Strain into a chilled coupe. —*Ezra Star*

Basil Gimlet

BASIL GIMLET

— MAKES 1 DRINK —

5 basil leaves, plus 1 small
basil sprig for garnish

1 oz. fresh lime juice

2¼ oz. London dry gin, such as
Martin Miller's

1 oz. Simple Syrup (p. 23)

Drop of celery bitters

Ice

This extraordinary twist on the traditional gimlet includes fresh basil and celery bitters. A long-lost type of bitters from the 19th century that has made a comeback in recent years, celery bitters are especially delicious in gin and vodka cocktails.

In a cocktail shaker, gently muddle basil leaves with lime juice, then add gin, Simple Syrup, and celery bitters. Fill shaker with ice and shake well. Fine-strain (p.20) into a chilled martini glass and garnish with basil sprig. —*Patricia Richards*

GINGER ROGERS

— MAKES 1 DRINK —

6 to 8 mint leaves, plus 1 mint
sprig for garnish

⅔ oz. Ginger-Pepper Syrup

1½ oz. gin, preferably Plymouth

¾ oz. fresh lemon juice

Crushed ice

2 oz. chilled ginger ale

The Ginger Rogers has been a best seller at San Francisco's Absinthe Bar & Brasserie since the day the place opened in 1998. The key is an intense ginger-pepper syrup that amps up the ginger ale flavor. "It's like a mojito dancing backwards in high heels," says former bartender Marcovaldo Dionysos.

In a chilled collins glass, muddle mint leaves with Ginger-Pepper Syrup. Add gin and lemon juice, then fill glass with crushed ice. Spin a swizzle stick or bar spoon between your hands to mix the drink. Stir in ginger ale, top with more crushed ice and garnish with mint sprig. —*Kathy Flick and Marcovaldo Dionysos*

GINGER-PEPPER SYRUP

Thinly slice a 1-inch piece of ginger. In a small saucepan, combine ½ cup sugar with 6 ounces water, 1 teaspoon whole black peppercorns, and ginger. Simmer over moderate heat, stirring, until sugar dissolves. Cook over low heat for 10 minutes. Remove from heat and let cool. Strain syrup into a jar, cover, and refrigerate for up to 2 weeks. Makes about 8 ounces.

DEATH AT THE SAVOY

¼ oz. absinthe

¾ oz. London dry gin

¾ oz. triple sec

½ oz. fresh lemon juice

Ice

1 oz. chilled sparkling wine

1 lemon twist, for garnish

According to mixologist John deBary, adding a splash of sparkling wine is one of the most reliable ways to augment a cocktail. Here, he has created something of a love child between the classic Corpse Reviver No. 2 (p. 37) and a Death in the Afternoon (absinthe and Champagne with a lemon twist).

Rinse a chilled coupe with absinthe and pour out the excess. In a cocktail shaker, combine gin, triple sec, and lemon juice. Fill shaker with ice and shake well. Strain into prepared coupe, top with wine, and garnish with lemon twist. —*John deBary*

TWO PALMS

————— MAKES 1 DRINK —————

1 oz. London dry gin, such as Beefeater

½ oz. fresh lime juice

½ oz. Simple Syrup (p. 23)

1 large egg white

Ice

1 oz. chilled coconut water

Pinch of freshly grated nutmeg, for garnish

Coconut water is the breakout beverage of the decade, but people were actually mixing it into cocktails back in the 1800s. New Orleans bartender Nick Detrich read about it in Jeff "Beachbum" Berry's *Potions of the Caribbean: 500 Years of Tropical Drinks and the People Behind Them*. "The recipe went something like, 'Crack an egg, drop it in the coconut. Shake it up and add some gin,'" Detrich recalls.

In a cocktail shaker, combine gin, lime juice, Simple Syrup, and egg white. Shake vigorously. Fill shaker with ice and shake again. Fine-strain (p. 20) into a chilled coupe. Stir coconut water into cocktail and garnish with grated nutmeg. —*Nick Detrich*

GREEN LANTERN

MAKES 1 DRINK

½ kiwi, peeled and diced,
plus 1 or 2 kiwi slices
skewered on a pick for
garnish

¼ oz. Simple Syrup (p. 23)

1½ oz. gin, preferably Hendrick's

1 oz. chilled Viognier

½ oz. fresh lime juice

Ice

Kiwi, a fruit often overlooked in cocktails, adds a lovely green hue to this drink created by New York City beverage director Thomas Waugh.

In a cocktail shaker, muddle diced kiwi with Simple Syrup. Add gin, Viognier, and lime juice; fill shaker with ice and shake well. Strain into a chilled martini glass and garnish with skewered kiwi slices. —*Thomas Waugh*

CDT SUNSET

MAKES 1 DRINK

3 mint leaves

¼ oz. Simple Syrup (p. 23)

½ oz. Pimm's No. 1
(gin-based aperitif)

½ oz. Campari

½ oz. peach liqueur, such as
Mathilde

½ oz. fresh orange juice

¼ oz. fresh lime juice

Ice

1½ oz. chilled Cava

Colorado bartender Bryan Dayton makes a juiced-up Aperol spritz using Campari, Aperol's more bracing cousin. The color of the drink reminds Dayton of beautiful sunsets he's seen from the Continental Divide Trail.

In a cocktail shaker, muddle 2 mint leaves with Simple Syrup. Add Pimm's, Campari, peach liqueur, orange juice, and lime juice. Fill shaker with ice and shake well. Fine-strain (p. 20) into a chilled flute and top with cava. Smack (p. 20) the remaining mint leaf over drink and add to glass. —*Bryan Dayton*

PIMM'S CUP

MAKES 1 DRINK

- 2 oz. Pimm's No. 1 (gin-based aperitif)
- 4 oz. chilled bitter lemon soda (see Note)
- Ice
- 1 lemon wedge, 1 apple slice, and 1 cucumber spear, for garnish

Wimbledon spectators drink ten to fifteen thousand Pimm's Cups every day. Americans often make the low-alcohol cocktail with Sprite or 7 Up, but Greg Best opts for the British way, using bitter lemon soda for "the perfect balance between sweet and tart."

In a chilled collins glass combine Pimm's and lemon soda. Fill with ice and stir well. Garnish with lemon wedge, apple slice, and cucumber spear. —*Greg Best*

Note

Schweppes and Fever-Tree make high-quality, widely available bitter lemon sodas.

About Pimm's No. 1

Pimm's No. 1 is a gin-based drink made in England from dry gin, liqueur, fruit juices, and spices. It was created in 1859 by the English oyster bar owner James Pimm. It has a dark, golden-brown color, a medium body, and a taste of citrus fruits and spice and is served either on the rocks or used in cocktails.

NORSEMAN

2 oz. Brown Butter–Washed Aquavit

1 tsp. Rich Simple Syrup (p. 23)

2 dashes of Angostura bitters

1 large ice cube

1 apple slice, for garnish

Andrew Volk, owner of Portland Hunt & Alpine Club in Maine, applies the popular mixology technique of fat washing here. He blends browned butter with aquavit, chills the mixture, then scrapes the re-solidified butter off the top. The "washed" aquavit takes on the brown butter's nutty flavor without any of the greasiness.

In a chilled double rocks glass, combine Brown Butter–Washed Aquavit, Rich Simple Syrup, and bitters. Add large ice cube and stir well. Garnish with apple slice. —*Andrew Volk*

BROWN BUTTER–WASHED AQUAVIT

In a small skillet, cook 3 tablespoon unsalted butter over moderately low heat until browned, 5 to 7 minutes. Pour through a fine strainer set over a small bowl; let butter cool. In a jar, combine 8 ounces aquavit with 1 tablespoon of the brown butter. Let steep at room temperature for 6 to 8 hours, shaking occasionally, then freeze until the fats solidify. Skim off any solids. Refrigerate the Brown Butter–Washed Aquavit for up to 4 weeks. Makes about 8 ounces.

About Aquavit

Aquavit is a Scandinavian neutral spirit distilled from grain or potato. It has much in common with gin, but rather than juniper as its essential element, aquavit's flavor comes from caraway and a blend of other herbs and spices. The signature spice of caraway makes aquavit a perfect pairing for traditional Nordic fare like pickled herring, smoked fish, and pungent cheeses. Use aquavit as you would gin or vodka.

PDT/Crif Frozen
Piña Colada, p. 70

Rum

Rum

Rum is always made from some form of sugarcane. Molasses is the most common, but any form can be distilled, from fresh cane juice to granulated cane sugar. Most rum is aged in wooden barrels, but some rests in stainless steel tanks before bottling. For rum aged in barrels, the length of time in the barrel dictates both flavor and color.

TYPES OF RUM

White A clear rum typically made from molasses and distilled to a very high proof for a clean flavor, this is the type most often used in cocktails.

Amber Amber (or golden) rums are aged a shorter time than dark rums and sometimes have caramel added for color.

Dark Aged for a long time, dark rum retains much of the molasses flavors that are left intact during the distillation process.

Rhum Agricole This rum is made from freshly pressed sugarcane juice instead of fermented molasses. An unaged product, it has a grassy, slightly funky flavor.

Spiced Rum Rich and robust, this type of rum is flavored with spices such as vanilla, ginger, clove, and cinnamon. It can be made in the same way as golden rum or can be a dark rum with added spices.

Cachaça The national spirit of Brazil, cachaça is made with fermented fresh cane juice instead of sugar by-products. Most of it is unaged and has a slightly grassy yet clean flavor, but it can also be made in pot stills and aged like other sugarcane-based spirits.

THE GEOGRAPHY OF RUM

Nearly every country in and near the Caribbean makes its own rum, and the geography often determines the style and the flavor.

English-Style English-speaking islands and countries are known for molasses-based rums that are darker in color and flavor. Countries include Barbados, Belize, Bermuda, Guyana, Jamaica, St. Lucia, and Trinidad and Tobago.

Spanish-Style The Spanish style of rum tends to be a smoother and lighter style, typically distilled from molasses. Countries producing this type of rum include Cuba, the Dominican Republic, Guatemala, Nicaragua, Panama, and Venezuela.

French-Style The French-speaking countries make rum (Rhum Agricole) from fresh cane juice, resulting in a product that is grassy, floral, and earthy. These areas include Guadeloupe, Haiti, Martinique, and Mauritius.

MOJITO

— MAKES 1 DRINK —

5 mint leaves, plus 1 mint sprig
for garnish

1½ oz. chilled club soda

Ice

1½ oz. white rum

¾ oz. fresh lime juice

¾ oz. Simple Syrup (p. 23)

The oldest-known recipe for the mojito appeared as the Mojo de Ron in a 1929 Cuban guide called *Libro de Cocktail (The Cocktail Book).*

In a chilled collins glass, muddle mint leaves with ½ ounce soda. Fill glass with ice. In a cocktail shaker, combine rum, lime juice, and Simple Syrup. Fill shaker with ice and shake well. Strain into prepared glass, stir in remaining soda, and garnish with mint.

QUEEN'S PARK SWIZZLE

— MAKES 1 DRINK —

2 oz. aged Demerara rum, such
as El Dorado 15-year

1 oz. fresh lime juice

½ oz. Rich Simple Syrup (p. 23)

Crushed ice or pebble ice
(slightly larger and more
rounded than crushed ice)

2 dashes of Angostura bitters

2 dashes of Peychaud's bitters

1 mint sprig, for garnish

This early-1900s lime-rum cocktail was born at Trinidad's now-closed Queen's Park Hotel. It is traditionally served over crushed ice and mixed with a swizzle stick.

In a chilled collins glass, combine rum, lime juice, and Rich Simple Syrup. Fill glass with crushed ice and spin a swizzle stick or bar spoon between your hands to mix the drink, then add more crushed ice. Top with both bitters and garnish with mint.

MAI TAI

— MAKES 1 DRINK —

1 oz. aged dark rum, preferably Jamaican

1 oz. aged Martinique rum, such as Rhum J.M

¾ oz. fresh lime juice, lime shell (half lime, juiced and turned inside out) reserved for garnish

½ oz. orange curaçao

½ oz. orgeat (almond syrup)

Crushed ice

1 mint sprig and 1 pineapple spear (optional), for garnish

Victor "Trader Vic" Bergeron created the mai tai in 1944 using a private stash of 17-year-old imported Jamaican rum. This recipe uses a blend of aged rums to approximate its flavor.

In a cocktail shaker, combine both rums, lime juice, curaçao, and orgeat. Fill shaker with crushed ice and shake well. Pour into a chilled double rocks or hurricane glass and garnish with the lime shell, mint sprig, and pineapple spear.

TIA MIA

— MAKES 1 DRINK —

1 oz. mezcal

1 oz. amber rum

¾ oz. fresh lime juice

½ oz. curaçao, preferably Pierre Ferrand Dry

½ oz. orgeat (almond syrup)

Ice cubes, plus crushed ice for serving

1 mint sprig, 1 lime wheel, and 1 orchid (optional), for garnish

Brooklyn bartender Ivy Mix riffs on a mai tai with smoky mezcal. The name of the drink (an anagram of "mai tai") pays homage to a friend to whom she used to serve drinks in Guatemala.

In a cocktail shaker, combine mezcal, rum, lime juice, curaçao, and orgeat; fill with ice cubes and shake well. Strain into a chilled, crushed ice–filled rocks glass. Garnish with mint sprig, lime wheel, and orchid. —*Ivy Mix*

Tia Mia

RUM & TONIC

2 oz. white rum, preferably
    Banks 5-Island

5 oz. chilled tonic water,
    preferably Fever-Tree
    premium Indian tonic water

2 dashes of lemon bitters

    Ice

1 lemon wheel, for garnish

Virginia mixologist Todd Thrasher says this cocktail puts
him in vacation mode. He's a longtime scuba diver, and
when he visits the Caribbean island of Bonaire, this is his
go-to drink after a day in the water.

In a chilled highball glass, combine rum, tonic water, and lemon
bitters. Fill glass with ice and stir well. Garnish with lemon wheel.
—Todd Thrasher

CLASSIC

CUBA LIBRE

———— MAKES 1 DRINK ————

1½ oz. white rum

  3 oz. chilled Coca-Cola

  1 tsp. fresh lime juice

    Ice

  1 lime wedge, for garnish

The best kind of cola to use in this drink is Mexican Coca-
Cola or another brand made with cane sugar. Sugar-based
colas have a crisper, cleaner flavor than the more readily
available ones made with high-fructose corn syrup.

In a chilled highball glass combine rum, Coca-Cola, and lime
juice. Fill glass with ice and stir gently. Garnish with lime wedge.
—Hidetsugu Ueno

DARK & STORMY

———— MAKES 1 DRINK ————

2 oz. dark rum, preferably Gosling's

½ oz. fresh lime juice (optional)

Ice

3 oz. chilled ginger beer

1 lime wheel, for garnish

Per Gosling's lore, this drink was invented more than 100 years ago when members of Bermuda's Royal Naval Officer's Club added a splash of the local rum to their ginger beer.

In a cocktail shaker, combine rum and lime juice. Fill shaker with ice and shake well. Strain into a chilled, ice-filled collins glass, stir in ginger beer, and garnish with lime wheel.

CABLE CAR

———— MAKES 1 DRINK ————

1 lemon wedge

Superfine sugar

2 oz. spiced rum

1 oz. fresh lemon juice

¾ oz. orange curaçao

Ice

1 orange twist, for garnish

Mixology consultant Tony Abou-Ganim created the Cable Car in 1996 for Harry Denton's Starlight Room, located "between the stars and the cable cars" (according to the slogan) on the top floor of the Sir Francis Drake Hotel in San Francisco.

Moisten outer rim of a chilled martini glass with lemon wedge and coat lightly with sugar. In a cocktail shaker, combine rum, lemon juice, and curaçao; fill shaker with ice and shake well. Strain into prepared martini glass and garnish with orange twist. —Tony Abou-Ganim

Desk Job

DESK JOB

¾ oz. amber rum, preferably Ron Zacapa 23

¾ oz. overproof Jamaican rum, preferably Smith & Cross

¾ oz. Punt e Mes (spicy, orange-accented Italian sweet vermouth)

¾ oz. Cynar (bitter, artichoke-flavored aperitif)

Ice

1 lime peel, for garnish

"This drink is like a really bitter, dense rum and Coke–it would be my go-to happy hour cocktail if I had a desk job!" says New York bartender Donny Clutterbuck.

In a mixing glass, combine rums, Punt e Mes, and Cynar. Fill glass with ice and stir well. Strain into a chilled, ice-filled rocks glass. Pinch the lime peel over the drink and add to glass. —*Donny Clutterbuck*

DILAPIDATED BEACH HOUSE

1 oz. Trinidadian rum, such as The Scarlet Ibis

1 oz. amber rum

1 oz. Coco López sweetened cream of coconut

1 oz. chilled brewed espresso

½ oz. Cardamaro (wine-based amaro)

½ oz. Cinnamon Syrup (p. 23)

½ oz. passion fruit syrup (available at specialty stores and from kalustyans.com)

Ice

1 orange twist and 1 cocktail umbrella (optional), for garnish

Espresso meets rum and passion fruit in this modern tiki cocktail that tastes like a boozy, exotic iced coffee. The drink's creator, Shannon Smith, says, "There is something delightful about it both on a sunny patio or in the dead of winter."

In a cocktail shaker, combine rums, Coco López, espresso, Cardamaro, Cinnamon Syrup, and passion fruit syrup. Fill shaker with ice and shake well. Pour into a chilled double rocks glass. Pinch orange twist over the drink and add to the glass. Garnish with cocktail umbrella. —*Shannon Smith*

HOT BUTTERED RUM

—— MAKES 1 DRINK ——

2 oz. dark or amber rum

¾ oz. melted ghee or unsalted butter

½ to ¾ oz. honey

4 oz. hot water

Freshly grated nutmeg, for garnish

Ghee (clarified butter) mixes with rum more easily than regular butter, giving this hot toddy a silkier texture. Ghee is available in jars at Whole Foods and specialty food markets as well as Indian groceries.

In a warmed mug or heatproof glass, combine rum with ghee and honey. Stir in hot water and garnish with nutmeg.

TOM & JERRY

—— MAKES 4 DRINKS ——

8 oz. Tom & Jerry Batter

4 oz. Cognac

4 oz. aged rum

8 oz. hot whole milk

Freshly grated nutmeg, for garnish

"It may seem like a bit of a nuisance to make such a labor-intensive drink," says bartender John Gertsen of this classic 19th-century eggnog. "But at the end of a long shift, there's nothing better than a nice, hot Tom & Jerry."

Pour Tom & Jerry Batter into a large heatproof measuring cup. Gently fold in Cognac and rum, then gently stir in hot milk. Pour into 4 small warmed mugs or heatproof glasses. Garnish with nutmeg. —*John Gertsen*

TOM & JERRY BATTER

In a medium bowl, beat 3 large egg whites with ⅛ teaspoon cream of tartar until soft peaks form. In another bowl, beat 3 egg yolks with ½ ounce aged rum. Gradually beat in 1 cup superfine sugar, ⅛ teaspoon ground cinnamon, ⅛ teaspoon ground mace, ⅛ teaspoon ground allspice, and a small pinch of ground cloves. Gently fold in beaten egg whites. The batter can be refrigerated overnight. Makes about 20 ounces.

Tom & Jerry

THE WITCHES' COFFEE

4 tsp. Demerara or other raw sugar

12 oz. hot brewed coffee

6 oz. amber rum, preferably Ron Zacapa 23

3 oz. Strega (saffron-infused liqueur)

Averna Cream, for garnish

To underscore the rich flavor of dark Sumatra coffee in this variation of Irish Coffee, Colorado mixologist Bryan Dayton mixes the coffee with aged rum, spicy, saffron-based Strega, and raw sugar. He spices up the whipped cream with bittersweet Italian Averna.

In a heatproof pitcher, stir sugar into coffee until dissolved, then stir in rum and Strega. Pour coffee into warmed mugs or heatproof glasses and spoon Averna Cream on top.
—*Bryan Dayton*

AVERNA CREAM

In a medium-size chilled bowl, whip 4 ounces chilled heavy cream with 1 ounce Averna amaro and ½ tablespoon granulated sugar until soft peaks form. Use the cream immediately. Makes enough for 4 drinks.

DAIQUIRI

— MAKES 1 DRINK —

- 2 oz. white rum
- ¾ oz. fresh lime juice
- ¾ oz. Simple Syrup (p. 23)
- Ice

Daiquiris often mean frozen drinks that are flavored with commercial sour mix and cheap rum. Leo Robitschek, the bar director at Eleven Madison Park and the NoMad Hotel in New York City, loves introducing people to the real deal: "They're shocked that three simple ingredients can create such a complex drink."

In a cocktail shaker, combine rum, lime juice, and Simple Syrup. Fill shaker with ice and shake well. Strain into a chilled coupe. —*Leo Robitschek*

HEMINGWAY DAIQUIRI

— MAKES 1 DRINK —

- 2 oz. white rum
- ¾ oz. fresh lime juice
- ½ oz. fresh grapefruit juice
- ½ oz. maraschino liqueur
- Ice
- 1 lime wheel, for garnish (optional)

Ernest Hemingway once wrote that daiquiris "felt, as you drank them, the way downhill glacier-skiing feels running through powder snow." The daiquiri that Hemingway liked best included grapefruit juice and maraschino liqueur.

In a cocktail shaker, combine rum, lime and grapefruit juices, and maraschino liqueur. Fill shaker with ice and shake well. Strain into a chilled coupe and garnish with lime wheel. —*F&W*

Daiquiri

BANANITA DAIQUIRI

4 oz. white rum

1½ oz. banana liqueur

1 oz. fresh lime juice

½ oz. Simple Syrup (p. 23)

2 ripe baby bananas (or
1 regular banana), plus
2 unpeeled banana slices
for garnish

4 coffee beans

2 cups ice cubes

Julio Cabrera has been serving this update on the Cuban classic since day one at The Regent Cocktail Club in Miami. He blends in whole coffee beans to balance the sweetness of the drink.

In a blender, combine all ingredients except the garnish and blend until smooth. Pour into 2 large chilled coupes and garnish each drink with a banana slice. —*Julio Cabrera*

AUTUMN DAIQUIRI

2 oz. amber or spiced rum

¾ oz. fresh lime juice

½ oz. chilled unsweetened
pineapple juice

¼ oz. Rich Simple Syrup (p. 23)

¼ oz. Cinnamon Syrup (p. 23)

Dash of Angostura bitters

Ice

"Originally from Cuba, the daiquiri is usually a warm-weather cocktail. This version from New York City mixologist Joaquín Simó features spiced flavors that are perfect for cooler months. According to Simó, though, the drink "remains true to its daiquiri roots: tart and refreshing."

In a cocktail shaker, combine all ingredients except ice. Fill shaker with ice and shake well. Strain into a chilled coupe. —*Joaquín Simó*

CAPRESE DAIQUIRI

— MAKES 1 DRINK —

4 cherry tomatoes

2 basil leaves

¾ tsp. balsamic vinegar

Pinch each of salt and freshly ground pepper

2 oz. white rum

¾ oz. Simple Syrup (p. 23)

¾ oz. fresh lime juice

Ice

Herbed olive oil and 1 mini mozzarella ball skewered on a pick with 1 cherry tomato and 1 basil leaf, for garnish

San Franciso bartender Mathias Simonis once tasted a chicken Caesar cocktail at a mixology seminar. Inspired to reinvent his own favorite salad, he created this savory Caprese Daiquiri, which can include fun garnishes like olives and pickled peppers.

In a cocktail shaker, muddle 4 cherry tomatoes with 2 basil leaves, vinegar, salt, and pepper. Add rum, Simple Syrup, and lime juice, fill shaker with ice, and shake well. Fine-strain (p. 20) into a chilled coupe and garnish with olive oil, mozzarella ball, cherry tomato, and basil leaf. —*Mathias Simonis*

AVOCADO DAIQUIRI

— MAKES 1 DRINK —

2 oz. white rum

2 oz. dark rum

2 oz. Simple Syrup (p. 23)

1 oz. fresh lemon juice

¼ Hass avocado, peeled and sliced

1½ tsp. half-and-half

1 cup crushed ice

"This drink has gone from ugly duckling to swan," says bartender Lucy Brennan. It took her years to perfect this banana daiquiri revamp, and then it became a best-selling cocktail at Mint/820, her (now-closed) restaurant and bar in Portland, Oregon.

In a blender, combine all ingredients. Blend until completely smooth, then pour into a chilled wineglass. —*Lucy Brennan*

Monkey Tail

MONKEY TAIL

1½ oz. chilled overproof Jamaican rum, preferably Wray & Nephew

1½ oz. chilled white rum

1½ oz. chilled fresh orange juice

1½ oz. chilled fresh lime juice

1½ oz. chilled Simple Syrup (p. 23)

1 oz. chilled banana liqueur

1 oz. chilled coconut rum

2 cups ice cubes

Micah Melton, beverage director of The Aviary in Chicago, gives this sophisticated frozen daiquiri an ultratropical flavor by combining overproof rum, coconut rum, and banana liqueur. To get the right consistency, chill all the ingredients before blending.

In a blender, combine all ingredients and blend until smooth. Pour into 2 rocks glasses. —*Micah Melton*

PAPAYA CALIENTE

MAKES 2 DRINKS

4 oz. white rum

2 oz. Simple Syrup (p. 23)

1 oz. fresh lime juice

1½ tsp. pastis, preferably Pernod

Six 1-inch chunks of ripe papaya

2 cups ice cubes

2 tarragon sprigs, for garnish

Miami bartender Julio Cabrera re-creates the flavors of *jugo de papaya con anis*, a popular weight-loss drink in the Dominican Republic and Puerto Rico. His rum-laced version here has no purported slimming effects.

In a blender, combine rum, Simple Syrup, lime juice, pastis, papaya, and ice and blend until smooth. Pour into 2 large chilled martini glasses and garnish each drink with a tarragon sprig. —*Julio Cabrera*

PDT/CRIF FROZEN PIÑA COLADA

— MAKES 4 DRINKS —

5 oz. fresh pineapple juice

5 oz. fresh lime juice

3 oz. coconut water

15 oz. chilled white rum, preferably Caña Brava

6 oz. frozen coconut puree, such as Perfect Purée of Napa Valley

3 oz. cane syrup

4 pineapple wedges and 4 cocktail umbrellas (optional), for garnish

Jeff Bell of PDT in Manhattan says a piña colada is his guilty-pleasure drink. He makes this superfresh, pineapple-y version in a slushie machine at Crif Dogs, the hot dog joint next to the bar. In place of the typical overly sweetened cream of coconut, Bell blends in coconut water and coconut puree (available frozen at specialty markets).

Mix pineapple juice, lime juice, and coconut water and pour into an ice cube tray. Freeze until solid, about 4 hours. Transfer ice cubes to a blender. Add rum, coconut puree, and cane syrup and blend until smooth. Pour into 4 chilled double rocks glasses or large coupes and garnish with pineapple wedges and cocktail umbrellas. —*Jeff Bell*

FROZEN DAISY

— MAKES 2 DRINKS —

3 oz. white rum, preferably Bacardí Superior

1 oz. yellow Chartreuse

1 oz. fresh lime juice

1 oz. Simple Syrup (p. 23)

4 dashes of Angostura bitters

2 cups ice cubes

14 mint leaves, plus 2 mint sprigs for garnish

Miami bartender Julio Cabrera says this drink is like a frozen mojito with complex, herbal flavors from yellow Chartreuse. The honey-sweetened French liqueur, made with 130 herbs, plants, and flowers, dates back to 1838.

In a blender, combine all ingredients except mint sprigs and blend until smooth. Pour into 2 chilled collins glasses and garnish each drink with a mint sprig. —*Julio Cabrera*

PDT/Crif Frozen Piña Colada

Imperial Bulldog

KNICKERBOCKER

MAKES 4 TO 6 DRINKS

10 oz. chilled amber rum, such as Zaya 12-year

9 oz. chilled Raspberry Stock

7 oz. chilled Simple Syrup (p. 23)

5 oz. chilled fresh lime juice

3 oz. chilled Grand Marnier

2½ cups ice cubes

Micah Melton, beverage director of The Aviary in Chicago, updates the 1850s classic Knickerbocker–considered to be the great-granddaddy of all tiki drinks. Melton says the best way to enjoy his shocking-pink frozen version is "by the pool in the largest vessel possible."

In a blender, combine all ingredients and blend until smooth. Pour into chilled rocks glasses. —*Micah Melton*

RASPBERRY STOCK

In a medium saucepan, combine 2 cups raspberries with 8 ounces water and bring to a boil. Remove mixture from heat, cover and let stand until cooled to room temperature, about 2 hours. Strain mixture into a jar and refrigerate for up to 4 days. Makes about 10 ounces.

IMPERIAL BULLDOG

MAKES 1 DRINK

5 raspberries, plus 3 raspberries skewered on a pick for garnish

Crushed ice

¾ oz. aquavit

¾ oz. cachaça

¾ oz. fresh lime juice

¾ oz. fresh pineapple juice

¾ oz. Simple Syrup (p. 23)

3 small pineapple leaves and 1 bottle of Underberg bitters (optional), for garnish

Imperial Bulldog is the first cocktail that Jane Danger created with Austin Hennelly, her former partner at Mother of Pearl in New York City. Danger admires his cheeky finishing touches, like the miniature bottle of Underberg bitters inverted in the beer glass. As the ice melts, the bottle slowly empties into the drink.

In a chilled Belgian beer glass or pilsner glass, muddle 5 raspberries. Fill with crushed ice. In a cocktail shaker, combine aquavit, cachaça, lime juice, pineapple juice, and Simple Syrup and shake well. Pour into glass and top with more crushed ice. Garnish with pineapple leaves and skewered raspberries, and invert the bottle of Underberg in the drink. —*Jane Danger*

CAIPIRINHA

MAKES 1 DRINK

1 small lime, cut into 6 wedges

1 Tbsp. Demerara or other raw sugar

Crushed ice

2 oz. cachaça

Caipirinha, Brazil's national cocktail, roughly translates as "little countryside drink." Its foundation is sugarcane-based cachaça, long considered a coarse peasant product. Now, excellent artisanal cachaças are widely available in the US.

In a chilled double rocks glass, muddle lime wedges and sugar. Fill glass halfway with crushed ice and stir well. Stir in cachaça, then stir in more crushed ice. —*John Lermayer*

MAIDEN NAME

MAKES 2 DRINKS

4 oz. cachaça

2 oz. unsweetened coconut cream (alternatively, skim the cream from a can of unsweetened coconut milk)

1 oz. fresh lime juice

1 oz. vanilla syrup (see Note)

Generous ½ oz. Cinnamon Syrup (p. 23)

Generous ½ oz. passion fruit syrup (see Note)

3 cups ice cubes

2 small pineapple leaves and freshly grated nutmeg, for garnish

"Who doesn't like coconut?" asks Ivy Mix of Leyenda in Brooklyn. "I mean, come on, I love piña coladas, but I always want a little more." She gives her version an extra flavor boost with passion fruit syrup, spices, and the sugarcane spirit cachaça.

In a blender, combine the cachaça, coconut cream, lime juice, vanilla syrup, Cinnamon Syrup, passion fruit syrup, and ice cubes. Blend until smooth. Pour into 2 chilled tiki mugs or pilsner glasses. Garnish with the pineapple leaves and nutmeg. —*Ivy Mix*

Note
Vanilla syrup and passion fruit syrup are both available at specialty stores and from kalustyans.com.

CAIPIRINHA MANCHADA

½ lime, cut into 6 pieces

¾ oz. Simple Syrup (p. 23)

1½ oz. cachaça

1 cup ice

½ oz. Hibiscus Agua Fresca

Greg Hoitsma of Andina in Portland, Oregon, transforms the caipirinha with fruity homemade hibiscus agua fresca. The name Caipirinha Manchada, which means "stained caipirinha," refers to the way the hibiscus agua fresca tinges the limes with crimson.

In a cocktail shaker, muddle lime pieces with Simple Syrup. Add cachaça and ice; shake well. Pour into a chilled rocks glass and float Hibiscus Agua Fresca on top, slowly pouring it over the back of a bar spoon near the surface of the drink. —*Greg Hoitsma*

HIBISCUS AGUA FRESCA
In a small heatproof bowl, steep 1 hibiscus tea bag in 8 ounces boiling water for 3 minutes. Remove tea bag. Add 8 black peppercorns, ½ teaspoon cardamom, ¼ teaspoon allspice, ¼ teaspoon cinnamon, and ¼ teaspoon cloves. Let cool. Strain Hibiscus Agua Fresca through a coffee filter into an airtight container and refrigerate for up to 1 week. Makes 8 ounces.

About Cachaça

Cachaça is essentially Brazil's version of rum. It's distilled from fresh sugarcane juice instead of sugar by-products and traditionally bottled without aging. This white spirit can be used in any drink that typically calls for white rum—and it's essential in Brazil's most popular drink, the caipirinha.

A Few Small Nips, p. 92

Tequila

Tequila

This spirit is a type of mezcal (much as Scotch and bourbon are types of whiskey) made from the blue agave plant; it is primarily produced in the area surrounding the Mexican city of Tequila, northwest of Guadalajara. Mezcal is defined as any agave-based liquor, which includes, but is not limited to, tequila. In total, mezcal is made from more than 30 varieties of agave. While "modern" tequila didn't come to be until the 1800s, mezcal dates back to the 1500s, when it was made by brandy-obsessed Spanish conquistadores. (See p. 91 for more information on mezcal.)

TYPES OF TEQUILA

Blanco Blanco, or silver, tequila is the most common take on the blue agave spirit. It is perfectly clear and can either be bottled directly after distillation or aged in steel tanks for up to 60 days.

Reposado This tequila is aged from two months to 1 year and is golden-colored, with subtle woody flavors.

Añejo Aged in wood barrels for one to three years, this tequila is smooth, with deep wood flavors. It is more expensive than other types of tequila and has a complex style that's better for sipping than mixing.

Joven Joven, or gold, tequilas are typically blanco mixtos that have had coloring and flavoring added prior to bottling. These tequilas are less expensive and commonly used for mixed drinks. However, joven tequila can also be the result of blending a blanco with a reposado or añejo in order to maintain the 100 percent agave classification.

TEQUILA TERMS

Agave Tequila, along with all other mezcals, must be made from agave. This desert plant is native to northern Mexico and the southwestern United States and includes hundreds of varieties. Tequila, however, requires blue agave, which thrives in the rich, volcanic soil of Jalisco. Blue agave is larger than most other varieties used for mezcal, and its core possesses a higher concentration of sugar, which makes it especially suitable for alcohol production.

Jalisco Jalisco is the central western Mexican state where 80 percent of all blue agave is grown. While laws have been relaxed so that tequila can be made in other Mexican states that don't include the actual town of Tequila, very few distilleries operate outside of Jalisco.

Mixto For a spirit to be tequila, it must be made from at least 51 percent blue agave. If the tequila contains anything less than 100 percent blue agave, however, it is considered to be a mixto. Many of us may have had our first tequila experience with a mixto and not even known it: Jose Cuervo Especial.

Normas Oficial Mexicana (NOM) Much like France's Appellation d'Origine Contrôlée, the Normas Oficial Mexicana (NOM) certifies that specific spirits meet the geographic and ingredient-based requirements of Tequila.

MARGARITA

—— MAKES 1 DRINK ——

2 lime wedges

Kosher salt

2 oz. blanco tequila

¾ oz. Cointreau or other triple sec

¾ oz. fresh lime juice

¼ oz. Simple Syrup (p. 23)

Ice

Arguably the most popular cocktail in the United States, the margarita is said to have been invented in the 1930s by the manager of the Garci Crespo Hotel in Puebla, Mexico. His girlfriend, Margarita, loved salt with her drinks.

Moisten half of the outer rim of a chilled coupe with 1 lime wedge and coat lightly with salt. In a cocktail shaker, combine tequila, Cointreau, lime juice, and Simple Syrup. Fill shaker with ice and shake well. Strain into prepared coupe and garnish with remaining lime wedge.

MARIA'S MARGARITA

—— MAKES 6 DRINKS ——

2 tsp. superfine sugar

2 tsp. cayenne pepper

2 tsp. sea salt

1 lime wedge

12 oz. blanco tequila

6 oz. Cointreau or other triple sec

6 oz. Cucumber Mix

12 Cucumber Ice Cubes

6 cucumber wheels, for garnish

The cucumber mix in this margarita from Virginia mixologist Todd Thrasher is used in two ways: It's shaken into the drink as a liquid and as ice cubes. The ice cubes, which are strained out, chill the drink without diluting its cucumber flavor.

On a small plate, combine sugar, cayenne pepper, and salt. Moisten outer rims of 6 chilled martini glasses with lime wedge and coat lightly with the sugar-spice mix. In a cocktail shaker, combine tequila, Cointreau, and Cucumber Mix; add Cucumber Ice Cubes and shake well. Strain into prepared glasses and garnish with cucumber wheels. —*Todd Thrasher*

CUCUMBER MIX & CUCUMBER ICE CUBES

In a bowl, mix the juice of 2 English cucumbers with 2½ ounces fresh lemon juice, 2½ ounces fresh lime juice, ¾ ounce Simple Syrup (p. 23) and ½ teaspoon salt. Reserve 8 ounces for the drinks; pour the rest into an ice cube tray and freeze. Makes 8 ounces Cucumber Mix and 12 ice cubes.

LA PICOSA

2 tsp. sugar

2 tsp. salt

1 tsp. cayenne pepper

1 lime wedge

1½ oz. blanco tequila

½ oz. ginger liqueur, preferably Domaine de Canton

½ oz. Jalapeño Agave Syrup (p. 192)

½ oz. fresh lime juice

1 cup ice cubes

The name of this frozen margarita revamp alludes to the drink's flavor (*picosa* means "spicy" in Spanish). Miami bartender Julio Cabrera adds a triple dose of heat with ginger liqueur, jalapeño-infused agave syrup, and a cayenne pepper–sugar rim.

On a small plate, combine sugar, salt, and cayenne. Moisten half of the outer rim of a chilled double rocks glass with lime wedge and coat lightly with spice mix. In a blender, combine tequila, ginger liqueur, Jalapeño Agave Syrup, lime juice, and ice. Blend until smooth and pour into prepared glass. —*Julio Cabrera*

BEET IT

2 oz. blanco tequila

1 oz. fresh beet juice

¾ oz. Simple Syrup (p. 23)

½ oz. fresh cucumber juice

½ oz. fresh lime juice

Ice

1 cucumber ribbon skewered on a pick, for garnish

"I've always felt tequila had a natural affinity for super-earthy ingredients," says San Diego bartender Lindsay Nader, who makes this refreshing cocktail with beets. "Try not to spill, because the stain can be more perilous than red wine!" she warns.

In a cocktail shaker, combine tequila, beet juice, Simple Syrup, cucumber juice, and lime juice; fill with ice and shake well. Strain into a chilled, ice-filled rocks glass and garnish with the cucumber ribbon. —*Lindsay Nader*

La Picosa

Little Squirt

PALOMA

—— MAKES 1 DRINK ——

2 lime wedges

Kosher salt

2 oz. blanco tequila

1 oz. fresh grapefruit juice

¾ oz. fresh lime juice

½ oz. Simple Syrup (p. 23)

Ice

1 oz. chilled club soda

Noted mixologist Philip Ward combines fresh grapefruit juice, simple syrup, and club soda to make his own grapefruit soda for this recipe. Alternatively, you can swap in a good-quality soda like San Pellegrino Pompelmo.

Moisten the outer rim of a chilled highball glass with 1 lime wedge and coat lightly with salt. In a cocktail shaker, combine tequila, grapefruit juice, lime juice, and Simple Syrup. Fill shaker with ice and shake well. Strain into prepared glass, stir in club soda, and garnish with remaining lime wedge. —*Philip Ward*

LITTLE SQUIRT

—— MAKES 1 DRINK ——

¼ tsp. each ground green, white, black and pink peppercorns (or 1 tsp. ground pepper from a premixed peppercorn medley)

4 tsp. kosher salt

1 lime wedge

Ice

One 1-inch square of red bell pepper

1½ oz. blanco tequila

¾ oz. yellow Chartreuse (honeyed herbal liqueur)

¾ oz. fresh lemon juice

¼ oz. mezcal

1½ oz. chilled Squirt or other grapefruit soda

New York City mixologist Jeff Bell makes this savory take on a paloma with red bell pepper. He amps up the pepper flavor with a salty rim that includes four kinds of peppercorns. For an easy shortcut, look for bottles of mixed peppercorns with built-in grinders.

On a small plate, mix ground pepper and salt. Moisten outer rim of a chilled collins glass with lime wedge; coat lightly with spice salt. Fill glass with ice. In a cocktail shaker, muddle bell pepper. Add tequila, Chartreuse, lemon juice, and mezcal. Fill shaker with ice, shake well, and fine-strain (p. 20) into prepared glass. Stir in grapefruit soda. —*Jeff Bell*

RED SANGRITA

— MAKES 6 DRINKS —

15 oz. tomato juice

7 oz. fresh orange juice

3 oz. fresh grapefruit juice

2 oz. hot sauce

1¼ oz. fresh lime juice

½ jalapeño (with seeds for a spicier drink)

1½ tsp. pepper

1 tsp. salt

6 shots of blanco tequila, for serving

In Mexico, this spicy, citrusy tomato drink is the traditional chaser to sip with good tequila.

In a large pitcher, combine all ingredients except tequila and stir until salt is dissolved. Let stand for 15 minutes (30 minutes for a spicier drink). Discard the jalapeño and refrigerate sangrita until chilled, about 2 hours. Stir well and pour into rocks glasses. Serve with shots of tequila alongside.

GREEN GODDESS SANGRITA

— MAKES 6 DRINKS —

4 oz. fresh cucumber juice

4 oz. fresh lime juice

3 oz. fresh jicama juice

3 oz. fresh ginger juice (from a 4-inch piece)

3 oz. fresh green tomatillo juice

Juice of ⅔ cup well-packed cilantro leaves (see Note)

3 oz. fresh Granny Smith apple juice

Juice of ¼ serrano chile

2 oz. honey, preferably wildflower

Pinch of salt

Freshly ground white pepper to taste

6 shots of blanco tequila, for serving

New York City mixologist Joaquín Simó created this spicy-sweet take on sangrita, the typically tomato-based chaser for tequila. "The combination of tequila and sangrita is designed to be sipped, not shot," Simó says. "It can be consumed pretty much any time you're relaxing with friends."

In a pitcher, combine the juices, honey, salt, and pepper; stir well. Refrigerate until well chilled, about 2 hours. Serve in chilled fizz glasses with tequila shots alongside. —*Joaquín Simó*

Note
To juice cilantro, run it in the juicer with a more fibrous ingredient like apple.

Green Goddess Sangrita

Prismatic Blade

CORTEZ JULEP

12 mint leaves, plus 1 mint sprig for garnish

1¼ oz. blanco tequila

½ oz. oloroso sherry

½ oz. Cocchi Americano (fortified, slightly bitter aperitif wine)

¾ tsp. Simple Syrup (p. 23)

Dash of Angostura bitters

Dash of orange bitters

Crushed ice

1 blackberry, for garnish

"The marriage of sherry and tequila might have been the golden discovery Cortez was looking for," says Houston bartender Bobby Heugel. The key to the combination in this crushed-ice drink is using a nutty oloroso sherry and a bold tequila, such as 7 Leguas Blanco.

In a chilled julep cup, muddle mint leaves. Add tequila, sherry, Cocchi Americano, Simple Syrup, and both bitters; fill with crushed ice and mix by spinning a swizzle stick or bar spoon between your hands. Top with more crushed ice and garnish with blackberry. Lightly smack (p. 20) mint sprig over drink, then add it to the cup as garnish. Serve with a metal spoon-straw.
—Bobby Heugel

PRISMATIC BLADE

1 oz. Ramazzotti amaro

¾ oz. añejo tequila

¾ oz. heavy cream

½ oz. triple sec

4 oz. freshly brewed hot coffee, preferably pour-over

For a pop-up event in San Francisco, New Orleans bartender Nick Detrich worked with local cult roasters Sightglass and Spitfire Coffee. Among the exceptional cocktails: this tequila-spiked take on Irish coffee. Detrich tops the drink with a triple sec whipped cream made in a shaker–the removable spring from a Hawthorne strainer whisks the cream into soft peaks. Detrich loves this cocktail as an after-dinner drink.

1 Fill a large saucepan with water and bring just to a boil; remove from heat. In a small saucepan, combine amaro and tequila. Place the small saucepan in the hot water, stirring occasionally, until heated through.

2 Meanwhile, remove the spring from a Hawthorne strainer (p. 18) and place it in a chilled cocktail shaker. Add cream and triple sec; shake until cream is softly whipped. Add the coffee to amaro mixture and stir well. Pour into a warmed mug and top with triple sec whipped cream. —Nick Detrich

MADAME AE-MA

2 oz. tequila, preferably Avión

1 oz. triple sec

1 oz. fresh lime juice

1 tsp. gochujang, plus more for rim

Ice

Gochugaru, for rim

PHOTO ON P. 204

A rim of gochujang (Korean chile paste) and gochugaru (Korean chile powder) creates warming layers of heat in this tart and spicy take on a margarita. You can order gochujang and gochugaru online or find them at your local Asian grocery store.

1 In a cocktail shaker, combine tequila, triple sec, lime juice, and 1 teaspoon gochujang in a cocktail shaker. Add ice and shake until chilled and diluted, about 20 seconds.

2 Using a small offset spatula, paint the rim of a chilled rocks glass with gochujang and dust with gochugaru. Fill glass with ice and strain drink over ice. —*Esther Choi*

ESPECIA DE PINYA

MAKES 1 DRINK

2 oz. reposado tequila

1½ oz. yellow tomato puree

1 oz. fresh pineapple juice

¾ oz. fresh lemon juice

¾ oz. fresh orange juice

1 tsp. sherry vinegar

1 tsp. extra-virgin olive oil

Pinch of ground sea salt

Pinch of ground pink peppercorns

½ tsp. diced habanero chiles, preferably grilled

Ice

1 pineapple wedge skewered on a pick with 1 yellow cherry tomato, for garnish

As a Bloody Mary nonfan, New York City bartender Pamela Wiznitzer set out to remake the tomato-based brunch staple. "I LOVE this recipe," she gushes. "It has intense spices, fruitiness, and loads of nutrients, too! It's like going through detox and retox simultaneously."

In a cocktail shaker, combine all ingredients except ice and garnish. Shake well. Fill shaker with ice and shake again. Fine-strain (p. 20) into a chilled, ice-filled highball glass. Garnish with skewered pineapple and cherry tomato. —*Pamela Wiznitzer*

Especia de Pinya

TIDE IS HIGH

1½ oz. unsweetened cashew milk

¾ oz. mezcal

¾ oz. reposado tequila

¾ oz. fresh pineapple juice

½ oz. fresh lime juice

1 tsp. sweetened condensed milk

Crushed ice

3 cashews and 1 orchid (optional), for garnish

New York City tiki specialist Jane Danger mixes up this tequila-and-mezcal piña colada variation. Instead of coconut cream, she uses cashew milk for a toasty, savory flavor.

In a cocktail shaker, combine all ingredients except ice and garnishes. Shake vigorously and pour into a chilled, crushed ice–filled pilsner glass. Garnish with cashews and orchid.
—*Jane Danger*

About Mezcal

The word "mezcal" comes from the Aztec word *mexcalli*, which combines *metl* (meaning maguey, a.k.a. agave) and *ixcalli* (meaning cooked). The literal translation of mezcal is "cooked agave."

Mezcal is not a type of tequila—tequila is actually a type of mezcal. Mezcal refers to any alcohol made from agave, whereas tequila is made from a single type of agave—Weber's blue agave, also known as *Agave tequilana*.

Though mezcal can be made from any type of agave, the most popular type is called Espadín. Mezcal made from a different type of agave—Tobala—is rarer and more expensive. This agave grows wild in canyons at extremely high altitudes under the shade of oak trees.

Much like true Champagne can only be made in the Champagne region of France, true mezcal must come from one of eight states in Mexico, the largest of which is Oaxaca.

Mezcal gets its smoky taste and smell from the way agave breaks down before fermentation. The agave is placed in a pit dug into the ground and filled with hot coals, where it sits for two to three days, acquiring its signature smoky essence.

Contrary to popular belief, the worm in mezcal isn't a worm but a larva. There are two types of larvae that are often added to mezcal: white-and-gold or red. The white-and-gold larvae live in the agave root, and the red larvae reside in the leaves. Despite the worms' prevalence among brands, they are not necessary. And no, they won't make you hallucinate. —*Michael Zukin; Kendra Kuppin*

GRAPES OF WRATH

———— MAKES 1 DRINK ————

1 oz. mezcal

¾ oz. fino sherry

¾ oz. Barolo Chinato

¾ oz. fresh lemon juice

½ oz. Vanilla Simple Syrup (p. 23)

Crushed ice

15 Concord grapes

¼ oz. Simple Syrup (p. 23)

Leo Robitschek, bar director at Eleven Madison Park and The NoMad Hotel in New York City, showcases fragrant Concord grapes in this cocktail. Barolo Chinato, a spiced fortified red wine, intensifies the drink's grapey flavor.

In a chilled highball glass, combine mezcal, sherry, Barolo Chinato, lemon juice, and Vanilla Simple Syrup. Fill glass with crushed ice and mix by spinning a swizzle stick or bar spoon between your hands. In a mixing glass, muddle grapes with Simple Syrup and pour over the drink. —Leo Robitschek

A FEW SMALL NIPS

———— MAKES 1 DRINK ————

1¼ oz. mezcal

½ oz. pear brandy, such as Clear Creek

¼ oz. yellow Chartreuse (honeyed herbal liqueur)

¼ oz. St-Germain elderflower liqueur

2 dashes of orange bitters

Ice

1 lemon twist, for garnish

PHOTO ON P. 76

Austin bartender Jessica Sanders took inspiration from a Frida Kahlo painting called *A Few Small Nips* when creating this drink. "Like Frida's great love story with Diego Rivera, the cocktail is fiery and tumultuous but also tender and fragile," she says.

In a mixing glass, combine mezcal, pear brandy, Chartreuse, St-Germain, and orange bitters. Fill glass with ice and stir well. Strain into a chilled coupe. Pinch lemon twist over drink and add to glass. —Jessica Sanders

ROSA AMARGO

1½ oz. mezcal

½ oz. Combier Pamplemousse Rose grapefruit liqueur

½ oz. French blanc vermouth, preferably Dolin

½ oz. Campari

Ice

1 grapefruit twist

To give mezcal a pleasant bitterness, Brooklyn bartender Jeremy Oertel stirs in grapefruit liqueur. The bitterness of Campari helps emphasize the grapefruit flavor.

In a mixing glass, combine mezcal, grapefruit liqueur, vermouth, and Campari. Fill glass with ice, stir well, and strain into a chilled martini glass or coupe. Pinch grapefruit twist over the drink and discard. —*Jeremy Oertel*

NAKED & FAMOUS

¾ oz. mezcal

¾ oz. yellow Chartreuse (honeyed herbal liqueur)

¾ oz. Aperol

¾ oz. fresh lime juice

Ice

"A big, aggressively smoky, and funky mezcal is key here," says New York City mixologist Joaquín Simó. He recommends Del Maguey's Chichicapa mezcal.

In a cocktail shaker, combine mezcal, Chartreuse, Aperol, and lime juice; fill shaker with ice and shake well. Strain into a chilled coupe. —*Joaquín Simó*

Bloody Mary, p. 107

Vodka

Vodka

Colorless and flavorless, vodka is defined not by what it's made of but by its distillaton process. This means vodka can be made out of anything that can be fermented–fruits, vegetables, grains, sugarcane, potatoes, sugar beets, honey, molasses, and maple syrup–but traditionally it's made with fermented potatoes or grains. In order for vodka to become vodka, it must be distilled to at least 190 proof (95% percent alcohol by volume or ABV).

VERSATILE VODKA

"Vodka" comes from the Slavic word for water, *voda*. It's disputed whether it was first produced in Russia or Poland, but now it's made in virtually every country. While vodka is generally considered flavorless, different vodkas do display subtle differences in flavor notes, fragrance, and sweetness.

Perhaps, because it is colorless and does not have a strong flavor, vodka might have once been considered the bartender's least-favorite spirit, but now it's being appreciated for its high-octane character and its ability to amplify the other flavors in a drink. "When it comes to mixed drinks, there's no end to what you can do with vodka," says bartender John Clement. "I have the recipes for about 1,000 vodka drinks in my head." Vodka's neutral flavor works well when there is already enough going on in a cocktail, and often bartenders want to focus on the flavors of the other ingredients rather than on the liquor.

Vodka is also great for infusing— you can use spices, herbs, fruits, and vegetables to create a uniquely flavored vodka to use in cocktails. To make an infused vodka, simply add the desired amount of vodka to a jar, then add the flavoring ingredient. Cover the jar, and let it stand at room temperature for two days or up to a week. Pour the mixture through a fine strainer into a clean jar and store at room temperature for up to a month.

The majority of vodka companies also offer several flavored vodkas including citrus, vanilla, berry, pomegranate, whipped cream, and even chocolate. Depending on the brand, the flavoring sometimes includes a small amount of sweetener.

11 ESSENTIAL VODKAS

For mixing into dirty martinis, splashing with soda, or spiking up any drink you can think of, vodka is a necessary bottle. Here are 11 brands to know and try:

1 Tito's Handmade Vodka

2 Grey Goose

3 Sobieski

4 Aylesbury Duck

5 Luksusowa

6 Ketel One

7 Russian Standard Vodka

8 Stolichnaya

9 Reyka

10 Absolut Elyx

11 ZU Zubrowka Bison Grass Vodka

—*Carey Jones*

DIRTY BLONDE

2 oz. vodka

¾ oz. Lillet blanc

3 green olives for garnish, plus ¼ oz. brine from the jar

Ice

This riff on a dirty martini is made "blonde" with the addition of Lillet blanc, an amber French aperitif wine with subtle hints of orange.

In a mixing glass, combine vodka, Lillet, and olive brine; fill with ice and stir well. Strain into a chilled martini glass and garnish with olives. —*Butter, Chicago*

MIRTO MARTINI

1 oz. orange vodka

¾ oz. mirto

¾ oz. fresh lime juice

½ oz. Cointreau or other triple sec

¼ oz. Simple Syrup (p. 23)

Ice

4 blueberries skewered on a pick, for garnish

This drink features mirto, a bitter myrtle berry digestif from the islands of Sardinia and Corsica. Sardinian chef and cookbook author Efisio Farris makes his own mirto, but bottled mirto is increasingly available in spirits shops.

In a cocktail shaker, combine vodka, mirto, lime juice, Cointreau, and Simple Syrup; fill shaker with ice and shake well. Strain into a chilled martini glass and garnish with skewered blueberries. —*Efisio Farris*

COSMOPOLITAN

——— MAKES 1 DRINK ———

2½ oz. lemon vodka

1 oz. triple sec

1 oz. chilled cranberry juice

1½ tsp. fresh lime juice

Ice

1 lemon twist, preferably spiral-cut (p. 20), for garnish

Many credit this iconic 1990s cocktail to Toby Cecchini, a former bartender at The Odeon in Manhattan. Cecchini, author of the memoir *Cosmopolitan: A Bartender's Life*, recalls creating the drink in 1988. Bartenders today still rely on his recipe, using just enough cranberry juice to provide the sheerest pink color.

In a cocktail shaker, combine vodka, triple sec, and cranberry and lime juices; fill shaker with ice and shake well. Strain into a chilled martini glass and garnish with lemon twist.

BLUEBERRY COSMOPOLITAN

——— MAKES 1 DRINK ———

8 blueberries, plus 3 blueberries skewered on a pick for garnish

2 oz. vodka

½ oz. St-Germain elderflower liqueur

½ oz. chilled white cranberry juice

½ oz. fresh lemon juice

½ oz. Simple Syrup (p. 23)

Ice

For anyone who wants to flaunt a love of cosmos, muddled blueberries tint this version a gorgeous hot pink. Patricia Richards developed the recipe for a spring-summer menu at Wynn Las Vegas's Parasol Down bar at the height of blueberry season.

In a cocktail shaker, muddle 8 blueberries. Add vodka, elderflower liqueur, white cranberry juice, lemon juice, and Simple Syrup; fill shaker with ice and shake well. Fine-strain (p.20) into a chilled martini glass and garnish with skewered blueberries. —*Patricia Richards*

Blueberry Cosmopolitan

VODKA GIMLET

— MAKES 1 DRINK —

2 oz. vodka

2 Tbsp. Rose's lime juice

Ice

Lime wedge, for garnish

Traditionally a gimlet is made with gin, but this vodka version is a good choice for those who don't care for gin. Lime juice or lime cordial? Bartenders are on both sides of the aisle when it comes to the proper way to make a gimlet. Some claim that the only way is to use a lime cordial like Rose's lime juice, and that if you make it with fresh lime juice it's technically a rickey. Others say that making a gimlet with fresh lime juice is the only way.

In a cocktail shaker, combine vodka and lime juice. Fill shaker with ice and shake well. Strain into a chilled martini or old-fashioned glass. Garnish with lime wedge. —*Vincenzo Marianella*

SKYLINER

— MAKES 1 DRINK —

1½ oz. vodka (preferably Cathead Honeysuckle)

1 oz. fresh grapefruit juice

½ oz. fresh lime juice

½ oz. Campari

½ oz. Simple Syrup (p. 23)

8 drops habanero bitters (preferably Bittermens)

Ice

1 oz. club soda

Lime wheel, for garnish

Cocktails are the life force of a New Orleans party, and the bar at the Ponchartrain hotel offers fantastic ones such as this refreshing grapefruit and Campari cocktail.

In a cocktail shaker, combine vodka, grapefruit juice, lime juice, Camapari, Simple Syrup, and bitters. Fill shaker with ice and shake well. Strain into a chilled, ice-filled collins glass and top with club soda. Garnish with a lime wheel and serve immediately. —*Bayou Bar, the Ponchartrain hotel*

MOSCOW MULE

½ lime, plus 1 lime wheel
for garnish

2 oz. vodka

Ice

4 oz. chilled ginger beer

Traditionally served in a frosty copper mug, the Moscow Mule helped vodka become popular in the US in the 1940s. Previously, one American cocktail book had described vodka as "Russian for 'horrendous.'"

Squeeze ½ ounce lime juice into a chilled copper mug or collins glass and drop in the spent lime shell. Add vodka, fill mug with ice, and stir well. Stir in ginger beer and garnish with lime wheel.

5 Small-Batch Vodkas to Try

It's no stretch to say that the hottest small-batch hooch going these days is vodka. In the past 15 years, the number of artisanal vodkas has proliferated beyond anyone's expectations. Here are five of our favorites:

Tito's Handmade Vodka
This vodka is made in the first legal distillery in Texas in an old-fashioned pot still, just like fine single-malt scotches and Cognacs. It's gluten-free and cheaper than most premium brands.

Deep Eddy Vodka
Made in Austin, this 10-times-distilled, charcoal-filtered newcomer is named for the oldest spring-fed swimming hole in Texas. Deep Eddy is bold and smooth and comes in seven flavors.

Aylesbury Duck Vodka
Legendary barmen Simon Ford and Dushan Zaric worked long and hard to perfect this product. Though it's only been around a short while, there's nary a high-end craft cocktail joint in America where you won't find it featured prominently behind the bar.

Reyka
A great vodka made in Iceland, Reyka is clean and remarkably smooth. It's made with "impurity free" glacial water, giving it a kind of clarity that makes it very mixable.

Woody Creek Signature Potato Vodka
Colorado-based Woody Creek Distillers boasts that they are the only vodka-making operation in the US that harvests their own potatoes and has them in the still the same day. Woody Creek vodka's got character, depth, and soul. —*Dan Dunn*

Suburban Anxiety

LEMON DROP

MAKES 1 DRINK

1 lemon wedge

Sugar

2 oz. lemon vodka

¾ oz. fresh lemon juice

½ oz. Simple Syrup (p. 23)

Ice

1 lemon twist

A riff on the classic vodka martini, this lemony cocktail was one of the most popular cocktails in the US in the later part of the 20th century.

Moisten the outer rim of a chilled martini glass with lemon wedge and coat lightly with sugar. In a cocktail shaker, combine vodka, lemon juice, and Simple Syrup. Fill shaker with ice and shake well. Strain into prepared glass and garnish with lemon twist.

SUBURBAN ANXIETY

MAKES 1 DRINK

1 oz. vodka

1 oz. Lavender Syrup

½ oz. fresh lemon juice

Ice

2 oz. dry sparkling rosé

1 lavender sprig, for garnish

Charmed by the idea of a lavender lemonade, Atlanta bartender Lindsay Ferdinand created this drink for a bridal shower. "It's bright, bubbly, and deliciously different with the hint of lavender–a perfect girls'-day-out drink, but secretly men love it too," she says.

In a cocktail shaker, combine vodka, Lavender Syrup, and lemon juice. Fill shaker with ice and shake well. Strain into a chilled coupe, top with sparkling rosé, and garnish with lavender sprig.
—*Lindsay Ferdinand*

LAVENDER SYRUP
In a small saucepan, bring 4 ounces water to a boil and stir in ½ cup sugar. Simmer until dissolved, about 2 minutes. Add 1 tablespoon dried lavender or 1 lavender tea bag and remove from heat. Steep lavender in the hot syrup for 10 minutes. Strain syrup into a heatproof jar, let cool, and refrigerate for up to 2 weeks. Makes about 6 ounces.

KAMIKAZE

— MAKES 1 OR 2 DRINKS —

1½ oz. vodka

½ oz. fresh lime juice

2 tsp. Cointreau or other triple sec

Ice

Often associated with high-octane shots and happy-hour specials, the kamikaze has a history that can be traced back to a bar on the American naval base in Yokosuka, Japan, during the late 1940s or early '50s. Today, famed mixologist Hidetsugu Ueno makes a less sweet version, using a higher ratio of lime juice to triple sec.

In a cocktail shaker, combine vodka, lime juice, and Cointreau. Fill shaker with ice and shake well. Strain into a chilled, ice-filled rocks glass or 2 shot glasses. —*Hidetsugu Ueno*

CELERY KAMIKAZE

— MAKES 1 DRINK —

1 lime wedge

Kosher salt

2 oz. pepper vodka

1 oz. fresh lime juice

1 oz. celery juice

½ oz. Cointreau or other triple sec

½ oz. Simple Syrup (p. 23)

Ice

Portland, Oregon, bartender Kevin Ludwig adds pepper vodka and celery juice to the typically sweet-tart kamikaze, giving it a spicy-savory kick.

Moisten half of the outer rim of a chilled coupe with lime wedge and coat lightly with salt. In a cocktail shaker, combine vodka, lime and celery juices, Cointreau, and Simple Syrup; fill shaker with ice and shake well. Strain into prepared coupe. —*Kevin Ludwig*

Kamikaze

Bloody Mary

BLOODY MARY

8 oz. chilled tomato juice

1½ oz. vodka

¼ oz. fresh lemon juice

½ tsp. Worcestershire sauce, plus more to taste

½ tsp. Tabasco, plus more to taste

Ice

Salt

Freshly ground pepper

1 celery rib, 1 lemon wedge, olive, and okra for garnish

These days Bloody Marys are garnished with anything from olives and pickles to lobster claws and bacon cheeseburgers. Las Vegas mixologist Craig Schoettler keeps it classic with celery and lemon wedges, but olives and okra are always a tasty touch.

In a chilled collins glass, combine tomato juice, vodka, lemon juice, Worcestershire sauce, and Tabasco. Fill glass with ice and stir well. Season with salt and pepper; garnish with celery rib and lemon wedge, or celery, lemon, okra, and olive. —*Craig Schoettler*

MORNING GLORY

2 oz. vodka

1½ oz. cold-brew coffee concentrate

1 oz. unsweetened almond milk

¾ oz. Rich Simple Syrup (p. 23)

½ oz. vanilla liqueur or syrup

Ice

Pinch of cinnamon, for garnish

"This recipe is a better variation on the espresso martini, which can be sickly sweet and unbalanced," says Pamela Wiznitzer of Seamstress in New York City. The almond milk makes the drink creamy but not too rich.

In a cocktail shaker, combine vodka, coffee concentrate, almond milk, Rich Simple Syrup, and vanilla liqueur. Fill shaker with ice and shake well. Strain into a chilled, ice-filled highball glass and garnish with a pinch of cinnamon. —*Pamela Wiznitzer*

SPARKLING YUZU GIMLET

2 Tbsp. sugar

2 Tbsp. hot water

2 cups lightly packed mint leaves, plus small sprigs for garnish

1½ cups lightly packed basil leaves, plus small sprigs for garnish

1 cup thinly sliced English cucumber, plus 8 spears for garnish

16 oz. chilled vodka

3 oz. yuzu juice

18 oz. chilled sparkling water

Ice

Top Chef winner Mei Lin makes her Asian-style gimlet in a large pitcher for easy entertaining.

In a small bowl, whisk sugar with hot water until dissolved. In a pitcher, muddle mint and basil leaves with sliced cucumber and sugar syrup. Stir in vodka, yuzu juice, and sparkling water. Serve in chilled, ice-filled collins glasses garnished with small sprigs of mint and basil and a cucumber spear. —*Mei Lin*

Note
Yuzu is a tart fruit about the size of a tangerine that mainly grows in Japan, Korea, and China. Because it is so tart, it's not meant to be eaten alone but used in recipes. Look for fresh yuzu in Asian markets from September through November, or use the frozen juice, also found in Asian markets.

BOOZY WATERMELON SLUSHY

12 oz. watermelon juice

4 oz. chilled vodka

2 oz. chilled Aperol

2 oz. chilled fino sherry

1 oz. agave syrup

¼ oz. fresh lemon juice

3 cups crushed ice

Thin watermelon wedges and black and white sesame seeds, for garnish

At Treasury in San Francisco, there's always something icy churning at the bar. "Slushies signal a good time," says beverage director Carlos Yturria, the brains behind this watermelon-based party starter, spiked with fino sherry and Aperol.

1 Pour watermelon juice into an ice cube tray and freeze until solid, about 4 hours.

2 In a blender, pulse watermelon ice cubes with vodka, Aperol, sherry, agave, lemon juice, and crushed ice until smooth. Add more agave if desired. Pour into 4 chilled glasses and garnish with thin watermelon wedges and black and white sesame seeds. Serve immediately. —*Carlos Yturria*

Make Ahead
The watermelon ice cubes can be frozen for up to 1 month.

Sparkling Yuzu Gimlet

Coco Cooler

COCO COOLER

2 oz. fresh watermelon juice

2 oz. coconut water

1½ oz. vodka

¾ oz. Zucca (rhubarb-flavored amaro)

½ oz. fresh lime juice

½ oz. Simple Syrup (p. 23)

Ice

2 oz. chilled club soda

1 watermelon spear, for garnish

"This cocktail is a riff on one of my favorite cold-pressed juices: a light-pink, super-hydrating concoction called Aloe Vera Wang," says San Diego bartender Lindsay Nader.

In a cocktail shaker, combine watermelon juice, coconut water, vodka, Zucca, lime juice, and Simple Syrup. Fill shaker with ice and shake well. Strain into a chilled, ice-filled collins glass. Stir in club soda and garnish with watermelon spear. —*Lindsay Nader*

WASABI GRASSHOPPER

6 oz. heavy cream

2 Tbsp. sugar

1½ Tbsp. wasabi powder

¼ tsp. salt, plus more for garnish (optional)

4½ oz. white chocolate, chopped

16 oz. skim milk

3 oz. vodka

2 oz. crème de menthe

Chicago mixologist Micah Melton gives his grasshopper variation a surprisingly delicious tweak with just a hint of wasabi. He churns batches of the drink in an ice cream maker so it's creamy and smooth, like a thick milkshake.

1 In a small saucepan, bring cream, sugar, wasabi, and ¼ teaspoon salt to a simmer over moderately high heat, stirring constantly, about 3 minutes. Whisk in white chocolate until melted. Remove from heat and strain mixture through a fine sieve into a large bowl. Let cool completely, about 30 minutes.

2 Whisk milk into mixture, pour into an ice cream maker, and freeze according to manufacturer's instructions. Fold in vodka. Pour 6 ounces of grasshopper base into each of 4 chilled double rocks glasses and top each drink with ½ ounce crème de menthe and a pinch of salt. —*Micah Melton*

WHITE RUSSIAN

—— MAKES 1 DRINK ——

2 oz. vodka

1 oz. coffee liqueur

1 oz. heavy cream

Ice

The Dude, played by Jeff Bridges in *The Big Lebowski*, makes his White Russians (or "Caucasians," in Dude-speak) with half-and-half. Lighter versions call for milk, but this recipe goes all the way in the other direction with heavy cream.

In a cocktail shaker, combine vodka, coffee liqueur, and cream. Fill shaker with ice and shake well. Strain into a chilled, ice-filled rocks glass.

MATCHA MILK PUNCH

—— MAKES 1 DRINK ——

2 oz. Sencha Vodka

½ oz. half-and-half

⅜ oz. cane syrup mixed with ⅜ oz. water

⅛ tsp. matcha green tea powder

Ice

Kenta Goto, owner of Bar Goto in New York City, uses two types of green tea in this creamy, milkshake-like cocktail: herbaceous sencha and tannic matcha green tea powder.

In a cocktail shaker, combine Sencha Vodka, half-and-half, cane syrup, and matcha; shake vigorously. Fill with ice, shake again and strain into a chilled tea cup. —*Kenta Goto*

SENCHA VODKA

In a liquid measuring cup, steep 1 tablespoon loose sencha tea in 8 ounces vodka for 5 minutes. Strain vodka into a jar and keep at room temperature for up to 1 month. Makes 8 ounces.

Matcha Milk Punch

Mint Julep, p. 122

Whiskey

Whiskey

Whiskey (also known as whisky) is a broad category of spirits made from fermented grain mash. The type of whiskey is determined by the region where it's produced and the grain used in the distillation process. Different grains produce different taste characteristics. Couple that with distillation methods that vary by region and producer, and you get a wide range of flavors, from sweet to spicy and from smooth to bold and smoky.

TYPES OF WHISKEY

Straight Whiskey is made from at least 51 percent of one grain (often barley, but also corn, wheat, or rye). US straight whiskey must be aged in new charred-oak barrels for at least two years.

Bourbon is a type of American whiskey made from a mash of at least 51 percent corn and aged in new charred-oak barrels. Contrary to popular belief, bourbon does not have to be made in Kentucky—although 95 percent of the world's bourbon is made there. To be labeled bourbon, it just must be made in the US.

Rye Whiskey is an American whiskey that follows all the same laws as bourbon except one: Rye whiskey must be distilled with a mash of at least 51 percent rye. It is usually drier and spicier in flavor than bourbon.

Tennessee Whiskey is straight whiskey distilled in Tennessee and filtered through maple charcoal before aging.

Irish Whiskey is the oldest whiskey in the world and has become synonymous with smooth. Today, it's distilled and aged in Ireland in wooden barrels for at least three years before bottling.

Scotch Whisky, spelled without the "e" and usually just called Scotch, is distilled from malted barley in Scotland and aged in oak barrels for at least three years. The barley is often dried using smoke from burning peat, which gives Scotch its signature smoky flavor.

Canadian Whisky is a broad category of whiskies that are fermented, distilled, and aged in Canada. Canadians usually ferment, distill, and age each grain separately, then blend to create a smooth final product.

Japanese Whisky has gained more attention in the US over the past 10 years and is made in a single-malt style with extended barrel aging.

COMMON LABEL DESCRIPTIONS

Here are some common phrases used on whiskey labels:

Single Malts are distilled, aged, and bottled by one distillery and made entirely with one kind of malted grain, usually barley.

Blended Malts combine two or more single malts from different distilleries.

Blended Whiskies contain a mixture of barrel-aged malt and grain whiskies.

Single Cask/Barrel Whiskies are bottled from a single barrel.

Cask-Finished Whiskies get a secondary aging in a different type of barrel, usually one that has been used previously to age something else such as port or sherry.

Overproof means that the whiskey (or other spirit) has an alcohol by volume (ABV) higher than the industry standard of 40% ABV.

Bonded means that the whiskey was made at a single distillery, by one distiller in the same calendar year, aged for at least four years in a federally bonded warehouse, and bottled at 100 proof.

MANHATTAN

MAKES 1 DRINK

2½ oz. bourbon or rye whiskey

1 oz. sweet vermouth

2 dashes of Angostura bitters

Ice

1 orange twist, for garnish

When making a Manhattan, purists insist on the classic rye, which has a spicy bite, while others prefer to use their favorite bourbon.

In a mixing glass, combine bourbon, vermouth, and bitters. Fill glass with ice and stir well. Strain into a chilled martini glass and garnish with orange twist.

ELI CASH

MAKES 1 DRINK

1½ oz. bourbon, preferably Old Forester

1 oz. Averna amaro

½ oz. Art in the Age root liqueur

Dash of chocolate bitters

Ice

1 orange twist, for garnish

This dark, rich cocktail from Charleston, South Carolina, mixologist Ryan Casey tastes uncannily like root beer. Casey, a fan of Wes Anderson movies, named the drink after Owen Wilson's man-child character in *The Royal Tenenbaums.* "It's a grown-up play on something familiar to us when we were kids," he says.

In a cocktail shaker, combine bourbon, amaro, root liqueur, and bitters. Fill shaker with ice, shake vigorously for 30 seconds, and strain into a chilled coupe. Pinch orange twist over drink and add to glass. —*Ryan Casey*

OLD-FASHIONED

—— MAKES 1 DRINK ——

2 oz. bourbon

¼ oz. Rich Simple Syrup (p. 23)

2 dashes of Angostura bitters

Ice

1 orange twist and 1 brandied cherry skewered on a pick, for garnish (optional)

According to cocktail historian David Wondrich, the old-fashioned is a direct descendant of the earliest known "true" cocktail, which in 1806 consisted of "a little water, a little sugar, a lot of liquor, and a couple splashes of bitters." While it's not traditional, some bartenders muddle a cherry into the drink or add one as garnish.

In a mixing glass, combine bourbon, Rich Simple Syrup, and bitters. Fill glass with ice, stir well, and strain into a chilled, ice-filled rocks glass. Pinch orange twist over drink, add it to glass, and garnish with skewered cherry.

PARLOUR OLD-FASHIONED

—— MAKES 1 DRINK ——

2 oz. overproof bourbon, such as Booker's

1 oz. rye whiskey

½ oz. Piloncillo Syrup

Dash of orange bitters

Dash of Bittercube Cherry Bark Vanilla bitters

Dash of Angostura bitters

Ice, plus 1 large cube or ball for serving

1 orange twist and 1 brandied cherry skewered on a pick, for garnish

In his quest to make the perfect old-fashioned, Minneapolis bartender Jesse Held concocted this bracing rendition mixed with Mexican brown sugar syrup. "It's strong enough to please the boozehounds and rich enough for those who want something after dinner."

In a mixing glass, combine bourbon, rye, Piloncillo Syrup, and all of the bitters. Fill glass with ice and stir well. Strain into a chilled rocks glass over the large cube. Pinch orange twist over the drink, add it to glass, and garnish with skewered cherry.
—*Jesse Held*

PILONCILLO SYRUP

In a small saucepan, combine 3 ounces piloncillo (Mexican brown sugar) with 3 ounces water. Simmer over high heat, stirring frequently, until the sugar is dissolved, about 3 minutes. Let cool, strain into a jar, and refrigerate for up to 2 weeks. Makes about 4 ounces.

Old-Fashioned

Rock 'n' Rolla

ROCK 'N' ROLLA

1½ oz. overproof bourbon,
   such as Booker's

1 oz. apple juice, preferably
   organic

¾ oz. fresh lemon juice

½ oz. pure maple syrup

¼ oz. St. Elizabeth allspice
   liqueur

2 dashes of Angostura bitters

Ice, plus 1 large cube
   for serving

Pinch of freshly grated
   nutmeg, for garnish

"I love this drink because it is so immensely accessible and easy to make," says Bay Area bartender Chris Lane. "Really it's just a bourbon sour with a little flourish of spice and apple." Lane's inspiration for the drink was a biodynamic local fresh apple cider.

In a cocktail shaker, combine bourbon, apple juice, lemon juice, maple syrup, allspice liqueur, and bitters. Fill shaker with ice and shake well. Strain into a chilled double rocks glass over the large cube and garnish with nutmeg. —*Chris Lane*

EVERGREEN TERRACE

2 oz. bourbon, preferably
   Johnny Drum Private Stock

¾ oz. Campari

½ oz. Strega (Italian herbal
   liqueur)

¼ oz. ginger liqueur

Ice

This bright, bittersweet bourbon cocktail is named for the street where the TV family the Simpsons live. "Anyone who gets the reference loves it," says mixologist Ryan Casey.

In a mixing glass, combine bourbon, Campari, Strega, and ginger liqueur. Fill glass with ice and stir for 30 seconds. Let rest for 30 seconds, then strain into a chilled coupe. —*Ryan Casey*

MINT JULEP

—— MAKES 1 DRINK ——

8 mint leaves, plus mint sprigs
for garnish

½ oz. Simple Syrup (p. 23)

2 oz. bourbon, preferably
overproof

Crushed ice

Kentucky cocktail loyalists say, with straight faces, that when a mint julep is made just right, you can hear angels sing. It's the official drink of the Kentucky Derby–nearly 120,000 mint juleps are served each year at Churchill Downs.

In a chilled julep cup or fizz glass, muddle mint leaves and Simple Syrup. Add bourbon and fill cup with crushed ice. Spin a swizzle stick or bar spoon between your hands to mix the drink. Top with more crushed ice and garnish with mint sprigs.

CHARLESTON SOUR

—— MAKES 1 DRINK ——

1¾ oz. bourbon, preferably
Bulleit

½ oz. Pineapple Vinegar

½ oz. fresh lemon juice

½ oz. Simple Syrup (p. 23)

Ice

¼ oz. Sercial Madeira

In this tribute to his hometown, Charleston mixologist Ryan Casey uses a DIY pineapple vinegar. Pineapples are displayed all over the South Carolina city as a symbol of hospitality.

In a cocktail shaker, combine bourbon, Pineapple Vinegar, lemon juice, and Simple Syrup. Fill shaker with ice, shake well, and strain into a chilled, ice-filled highball glass. Float Madeira on top, slowly pouring it over the back of a bar spoon near the drink's surface. —*Ryan Casey*

PINEAPPLE VINEGAR

In a medium saucepan, simmer 4 ounces unsweetened pineapple juice over high heat until reduced by half, about 7 minutes. Remove from heat and stir in 6 ounces white vinegar and ¼ cup sugar. Let stand until sugar completely dissolves, about 10 minutes. Pour infused vinegar into a jar and refrigerate for up to 3 weeks. Makes about 9 ounces.

Mint Julep

Bourbon Chai
Milk Punch

SHARK EYE

MAKES 1 DRINK

1½ oz. bourbon, preferably Elijah Craig 12-year

¾ oz. passion fruit syrup (available at specialty stores and from kalustyans.com)

¾ oz. fresh lemon juice

½ oz. bonded rye whiskey

¼ oz. Luxardo maraschino liqueur

⅛ oz. curaçao

2 dashes of tiki bitters

Crushed ice

Small pineapple leaves (optional) and 3 dashes of Peychaud's bitters, for garnish

Bourbon and rye give a potent kick to this playful cocktail. At Mother of Pearl in New York City, Jane Danger serves the drink in a shark mug garnished with two thin pineapple fronds arranged to look like a fish. "Shark Eye can make you feel that island vibe on any occasion," Danger says. "Manhattan is an island, right?"

In a cocktail shaker, combine all ingredients except ice and garnishes. Shake well and pour into a chilled, crushed ice–filled shark mug or rocks glass. Garnish with pineapple leaves and Peychaud's bitters. —*Jane Danger*

BOURBON CHAI MILK PUNCH

MAKES 1 DRINK

2 oz. Chai Bourbon

¾ oz. heavy cream

½ oz. pure maple syrup

¼ oz. Simple Syrup (p. 23)

Ice

Kenta Goto, owner of New York City's Bar Goto, infuses bourbon with chai tea, then shakes the drink with cream and maple syrup. The result is like a boozy chai latte.

In a cocktail shaker, combine Chai Bourbon, cream, maple syrup, and Simple Syrup; shake vigorously. Fill shaker with ice and shake again. Strain into a chilled coupe. —*Kenta Goto*

CHAI BOURBON
In a jar, steep 1 tablespoon loose chai tea in 8 ounces bourbon for 1 hour. Strain and keep at room temperature for up to 1 month. Makes 8 ounces.

ROB ROY

—— MAKES 1 DRINK ——

2½ oz. blended Scotch

1 oz. sweet vermouth

2 dashes of Angostura bitters

Ice

1 lemon twist, for garnish

This cocktail is named after the Scottish folk hero Rob Roy. It's similar to a Manhattan but uses Scotch instead of bourbon or rye whiskey.

In a mixing glass, combine Scotch, sweet vermouth, and bitters. Fill glass with ice and stir well. Strain into a chilled martini glass and garnish with lemon twist.

CLASSIC

RUSTY NAIL

—— MAKES 1 DRINK ——

Ice

1 oz. blended Scotch

1 oz. Drambuie (honeyed Scotch-based liqueur)

1 lemon twist, for garnish

This is Seattle mixologist Anu Elford's recipe for a classic Rusty Nail: a 1:1 Scotch–Drambuie ratio. Since Drambuie is quite sweet, though, Apte sometimes uses 2 ounces of Scotch and ½ to ¾ ounce of honey liqueur. "People should experiment with ratios," she says.

Fill a chilled rocks glass three-quarters full with ice. Add Scotch and Drambuie and stir well. Garnish with lemon twist.
—Anu Elford

THE ADVENTURES OF PETE & PEACH

1 oz. peated Scotch, such as Ardbeg

1 oz. peach brandy

¾ oz. fresh lemon juice

¾ oz. Simple Syrup (p. 23)

1 large egg white

Ice

New York City mixologist Nick Bennett combines peach brandy with a peated Scotch, shaking in egg white for a fabulous richness. The peat in the Scotch yields love-it or hate-it reactions: Comparisons range from butterscotch to Band-Aids.

In a cocktail shaker, combine Scotch, peach brandy, lemon juice, Simple Syrup, and egg white; shake vigorously. Fill shaker with ice and shake again. Fine-strain (p. 20) into a chilled rocks glass. —Nick Bennett

BITTER SCOTSMAN

2 oz. blended Scotch, such as Chivas Regal

¾ oz. orgeat (almond syrup)

¾ oz. fresh lemon juice

½ oz. Campari

Ice

1 lemon wheel and a pinch of ground cinnamon, for garnish

"I thought a lot about the nuances of mole for this drink," says San Diego bartender Meghan Eastman. She combines sweetness and spice with a hint of smoke, echoing the flavors of the robust Mexican sauce.

In a cocktail shaker, combine Scotch, orgeat, lemon juice, and Campari. Fill shaker with ice and shake well. Strain into a chilled, ice-filled rocks glass and garnish with lemon wheel and cinnamon. —Meghan Eastman

BLOOD & SAND

—— MAKES 1 DRINK ——

1 oz. single-malt Scotch

¾ oz. Carpano Antica Formula
   or other sweet vermouth

¾ oz. Heering cherry liqueur

¾ oz. fresh orange juice

Ice

Debuting around the same time as the silent film *Blood and Sand*, starring Rudolph Valentino, this 1920s cocktail is smoky and fruity but not overly sweet, thanks to Heering cherry liqueur. Unlike most cherry liqueurs, it's slightly dry and tart.

In a cocktail shaker combine Scotch, vermouth, cherry liqueur, and orange juice. Fill shaker with ice and shake well. Strain into a chilled coupe. —*Lydia Reissmueller*

KILT & JACKET

—— MAKES 1 DRINK ——

2 oz. Highland Scotch

¾ oz. fino sherry

¼ oz. maraschino liqueur

2 dashes of orange bitters

Ice

1 brandied cherry, for garnish

"A Tuxedo No. 2 is a delicious cocktail, but I wanted to improve on that classic," says New York City bartender Nick Bennett. In place of the gin and vermouth, he adds Highland Scotch (a typically smoky single malt, such as Glenmorangie) and nutty fino sherry.

In a mixing glass, combine Scotch, sherry, maraschino liqueur, and bitters. Fill glass with ice and stir well. Strain into a chilled coupe and garnish with cherry. —*Nick Bennett*

SHORTER, FASTER, LOUDER

7 basil leaves

1¼ oz. blended Scotch

¼ oz. peated single-malt Scotch, preferably Lagavulin 16-year

¾ oz. Coco López sweetened cream of coconut

½ oz. green Chartreuse (herbal liqueur)

½ oz. fresh lemon juice

½ oz. fresh pineapple juice

3 ice cubes, plus crushed ice for serving

Dash of Angostura bitters

1 mint sprig, for garnish

"I love this drink because it's this really weird piña colada variation," says former Philadelphia bartender Sara Justice. When guests order it, she says, "it's fun to see them get excited about a drink that tastes different from the classic flavors they're expecting."

In a cocktail shaker, muddle basil. Add Scotches, Coco López, Chartreuse, and juices. Fill with ice cubes and shake well. Strain into a chilled, crushed ice–filled collins glass. Float Angostura on top, dashing it over the back of a bar spoon near the drink's surface. Garnish with mint sprig. —*Sara Justice*

443 SPECIAL

1 oz. Highland Scotch, such as Glenmorangie

½ oz. peated Scotch, such as Laphroaig

¾ oz. yellow Chartreuse

¾ oz. Amaro CioCiaro

Ice

1 lemon twist, for garnish

The 443 Special has become Nick Bennett's signature cocktail. He created it when he was working at Amor y Amargo in New York City. Bennett, now at NYC's Porchlight, says people still ask him to make this smoky Scotch drink laced with honey-sweetened yellow Chartreuse.

In a mixing glass, combine both Scotches, Chartreuse, and Amaro. Fill glass with ice, stir well, and strain into a chilled coupe. Pinch lemon twist over drink and add to coupe. —*Nick Bennett*

Sazerac

SAZERAC

MAKES 1 DRINK

¼ oz. absinthe

2 oz. bonded rye whiskey,
preferably Rittenhouse 100

½ tsp. Rich Simple Syrup
(p. 23)

3 dashes of Peychaud's bitters

Ice

1 lemon twist

"This drink was originally made with Cognac," says Chicago mixologist Mike Ryan. "But after the grape-killing phylloxera epidemic in France all but wiped out Cognac production in the 1870s, bartenders replaced Cognac with American-made rye whiskey." The recipe here is for the "modern" (rye-based) Sazerac.

Rinse a chilled rocks glass with absinthe and pour out the excess. In a pint glass, combine whiskey, Rich Simple Syrup, and Peychaud's bitters. Fill pint glass with ice and stir well. Strain into prepared rocks glass, pinch twist over drink, and discard twist.
—*Mike Ryan*

CLASSIC

IRISH COFFEE

MAKES 1 DRINK

2 tsp. light brown sugar

3 oz. hot brewed coffee

1½ oz. Irish whiskey, preferably
Bushmills

Dollop of unsweetened
whipped cream, for garnish

San Francisco's Buena Vista restaurant claims to have made America's first Irish coffee, in 1952. One of their patrons, a travel writer named Stanton Delaplane, helped them re-create the recipe after tasting the drink at Shannon Airport in Ireland.

In a warmed mug or heatproof glass, stir sugar into coffee until dissolved. Stir in whiskey, then garnish with whipped cream.

IN COLD BLOOD

1 oz. rye whiskey, such as Old Overholt

1 oz. Carpano Antica Formula or other sweet vermouth

1 oz. Cynar (bitter artichoke aperitif)

1 large ice cube

1 lemon twist and a small pinch of salt (optional), for garnish

This drink, according to Portland, Maine, bartender Andrew Volk, is "approachable but geeky with the salt"–which he adds to balance the bitterness of the artichoke-flavored aperitif Cynar. As pictured on the right, the drink starts with a shot of whiskey.

In a chilled double rocks glass, combine whiskey, vermouth, and Cynar. Add large ice cube and stir well. Pinch lemon twist over the drink and add to glass. Garnish with pinch of salt.
—Andrew Volk

JACK & JUICE

4 oz. fresh pineapple juice

1½ oz. Tennessee whiskey, preferably Jack Daniel's

1 oz. fresh pear juice

½ oz. fresh lemon juice

½ oz. fresh ginger juice (from a 1½-inch piece of ginger)

¾ tsp. honey

Ice

3 small pineapple leaves (optional) and 1 maraschino cherry skewered on a pick, for garnish

Lindsay Nader, a founder of Juice Saves juice bar in San Diego, created this drink with Eric Tecosky of Tennessee whiskey distillery Jack Daniel's. They revamp a basic sour by adding sweet pear juice and a good dose of zingy ginger juice.

In a cocktail shaker, combine pineapple juice, whiskey, pear juice, lemon juice, ginger juice, and honey. Fill shaker with ice and shake well. Strain into a chilled, ice-filled rocks glass and garnish with pineapple leaves and skewered cherry.
—Lindsay Nader; Eric Tecosky

The Circle of the Sun

THE CIRCLE OF THE SUN

1½ oz. 12-year Japanese whisky, preferably Hakushu

1 oz. dry vermouth, preferably Dolin

½ oz. pear liqueur

Ice

1 lemon twist, for garnish

"I was looking to make a spirituous cocktail, but one that isn't a punch-you-in-the-mouth drink," says Denver bartender Jason Patz. He lightens Japanese whisky with vermouth and pear liqueur in this four-ingredient drink.

In a mixing glass, combine whisky, vermouth, and pear liqueur. Fill glass with ice, stir well, and strain into a chilled coupe. Pinch lemon twist over drink and add to coupe. —*Jason Patz*

THE WAY OF THE SWORD

1 oz. 12-year Japanese whisky, preferably Yamazaki

¾ oz. sweet vermouth, preferably Dolin rouge

½ oz. Cynar (bitter artichoke aperitif)

¼ oz. ruby port, preferably Sandeman Founders Reserve

Ice, plus 1 large cube for serving

1 orange twist

Denver bartender Jason Patz riffs on a Rob Roy with Japanese whisky (the classic uses Scotch). He prefers Yamazaki 12-year, which is aged in bourbon casks, sherry casks, and Japanese oak barrels. While Japanese whisky distillers are free to mix and match casks, Scotch must be aged only in oak for at least three years.

In a mixing glass, combine whisky, vermouth, Cynar, and port. Fill glass with ice, stir well, and strain into a chilled double rocks glass over the large ice cube. Pinch orange twist over drink and discard. —*Jason Patz*

MATCHA HIGHBALL

2 oz. 12-year Japanese whisky, preferably Hibiki

½ oz. fresh lemon juice

½ oz. Honey Syrup (p. 23)

¼ tsp. matcha green-tea powder

Ice

4 oz. chilled club soda

1 lemon wheel, for garnish

A trip to Japan inspired Denver bartender Jason Patz to combine matcha (a vivid green-tea powder) with Japanese whisky. Matcha tends to clump when mixed with liquid; to loosen any that's stuck to the side of the shaker, swirl the club soda in the shaker before pouring it into the glass.

In a cocktail shaker, combine whisky, lemon juice, Honey Syrup, and matcha; shake vigorously. Pour into a chilled, ice-filled collins glass. Pour club soda into the shaker, swirl around to rinse, then stir into glass. Garnish with lemon wheel. —*Jason Patz*

DOUBLE-BARREL FIZZ

1¾ oz. Rittenhouse 100-proof rye whiskey

¾ oz. fresh lemon juice

¾ oz. Cherry Gastrique, plus 3 rehydrated gastrique cherries skewered on a pick, for garnish

¼ oz. Cinnamon Syrup (p. 23)

2 dashes of Angostura bitters

Ice

1½ oz. chilled sour red ale

While most fizz cocktails get their bubbles from seltzer or club soda, Bay Area bartender Chris Lane tops his drink with sour beer. Lane especially loves Rodenbach Grand Cru, which has a tart fruitiness that's exceptional with his tangy cherry gastrique.

In a cocktail shaker, combine whiskey, lemon juice, Cherry Gastrique, Cinnamon Syrup, and bitters; fill with ice and shake well. Strain into a chilled, ice-filled double rocks glass. Stir in ale and garnish with cherries. —*Chris Lane*

CHERRY GASTRIQUE
In a saucepan, mix 6 ounces tart cherry juice, ¾ cup turbinado sugar, ¾ cup tart dried cherries, 4 ounces white balsamic vinegar, and a pinch of salt. Simmer over moderate heat for 10 minutes. Let cool. Strain into a jar; reserve rehydrated cherries. Refrigerate gastrique and cherries separately for up to 3 weeks. Makes 8 ounces.

Matcha Highball

Clementine 75, p. 145

Wine

Wine

Wine, including sparkling and fortified, has its place in the world of cocktails. There are a number of advantages to using wine instead of spirits in cocktails: versatile flavors and levels of acidity, natural aromas, and lower alcohol content. Wine can either be the base ingredient, or it can play a supporting role in a cocktail that also includes another type of spirit. Light, dry, and low-proof wine cocktails are often served as aperitifs or for brunch, while cocktails featuring a fortified wine are good choices for after-dinner drinks or nightcaps.

TYPES OF WINES USED IN COCKTAILS

Sparkling Wine Significant levels of carbon dioxide give these wines their fizz. The best-known example of a sparkling wine is Champagne, which is produced exclusively in the Champagne region of France. Usually sparkling wine is white or rosé, but there are examples of red sparkling wines. The sweetness of sparkling wine can range from very dry brut styles to sweeter doux varieties. Cava is a sparkling wine that comes from Spain, and Prosecco is a sparkling wine produced in Italy. As a general guideline, most Champagne cocktails are best with a dry style, since most cocktails call for other sweet ingredients.

Sherry A classic fortified wine from Spain's Jerez region, sherry is made in several different styles. Fino and manzanilla sherries are the lightest and are crisp, salty, and unaged. Amontillado and oloroso sherries are dry, but have more flavors of dried fruits and nuts due to the extended oxidation. If the recipe does not specify which type of sherry to use, your best choice will be a dry sherry.

Vermouth This fortified wine is traditionally made bitter with wormwood and given its aroma by other spices and herbs. There are several styles of vermouth, including dry, sweet, or red, and blanc or white. Dry vermouth is a staple in martinis (p. 32); sweet vermouth is often used for Manhattans (p. 117). Italian bianco and French blanc are slightly sweeter than dry vermouth; rosé and rosato vermouths are pink, with a slightly spicy flavor.

Brandy Brandies are distilled from a fermented mash of fruit. Two of the most popular types of brandy are made from grapes and named for the regions in France where they are made— Cognac and Armagnac. Calvados is a brandy made from apples and sometimes pears in the Normandy region of France. Legally, brandy must be distilled at less than 190 proof and bottled at more than 80 proof.

Pisco This spirit is a colorless or yellow-to-amber grape brandy made in the wine-making regions of Chile and Peru. These two countries have a longstanding rivalry about who gets to call pisco their own. The classic cocktail made with this brandy is a Pisco Sour (p. 162).Unlike French brandies, pisco is not aged in barrels, so it's clear, not brown.

CHAMPAGNE COCKTAIL

— MAKES 1 DRINK —

1 sugar cube

3 dashes of Angostura bitters

5 oz. chilled brut Champagne

1 lemon twist, for garnish

According to master mixologist Dale DeGroff, this is one of the few original cocktails that appeared in the first (1862) version of the seminal *How to Mix Drinks* by Jerry Thomas. The recipe has remained unchanged for 150 years.

In a small dish or glass, soak sugar cube with Angostura bitters. Fill a chilled flute with Champagne, then add bitters-soaked sugar cube. Garnish with lemon twist. —*Jamie Boudreau*

TROPICAL MIMOSA

— MAKES 2 DRINKS —

5⅓ oz. pineapple juice

1½ oz. ginger liqueur

Chilled Champagne or sparkling wine, for topping

The classic mimosa, a mainstay of brunch menus, is usually made with fresh orange juice. This version takes a tropical turn and features pineapple juice and ginger liqueur.

Divide pineapple juice and ginger liqueur between 2 chilled Champagne flutes. Fill with Champagne and serve. —*Grace Parisi*

BELLINI

—— MAKES 1 DRINK ——

4½ oz. chilled Prosecco

1 oz. white peach puree

½ oz. crème de framboise
(raspberry liqueur)

Giuseppe Cipriani first served this cocktail in 1945 to use up an excess supply of fresh white peaches at his Harry's Bar in Venice. Three years later, Cipriani named the drink for the Renaissance painter Giovanni Bellini during an exhibition of the artist's work.

In a pint glass, slowly stir Prosecco into peach puree. Drizzle in crème de framboise, then pour into a chilled flute.

22 PUNCH

—— MAKES 1 DRINK ——

1 oz. amber rum

1 oz. tawny port

½ oz. fresh lemon juice,
strained

½ oz. Orange-Cinnamon Syrup

Ice

2 oz. chilled Champagne

1 edible flower, such as
nasturtium or pansy, or
nutmeg, for garnish

PHOTO ON P. 243

The potent 22 Punch is one of the hallmark tiki drinks at Chris and Anu Elford's bar, Navy Strength, in Seattle. The orange-cinnamon syrup that sweetens this cocktail is also delicious in a mug of tea and over vanilla ice cream.

In a cocktail shaker, combine rum, port, lemon juice, and syrup. Fill shaker with ice and shake to chill but not dilute, about 5 shakes. Place a few large ice cubes in a punch cup and strain drink over ice. Top with Champagne and garnish with a flower. —*Chris and Anu Elford*

ORANGE-CINNAMON SYRUP

Place zest of 2 oranges in a heatproof 16-ounce jar and add 1 cup sugar. Seal jar and shake to combine. Let stand at room temperature for 12 hours. Bring 1 cup water and 1 cinnamon stick to a boil in a saucepan. Pour into jar and stir to dissolve sugar. Let cool to room temperature, about 1 hour. Strain syrup and stir in a pinch of salt. Store in sealed jar in refrigerator up to 1 month. Makes about 8 ounces.

CLEMENTINE 75

½ cup sugar

One 3-inch piece of fresh ginger, thinly sliced

¼ cup juniper berries, crushed

¼ cup dried cranberries

2 cinnamon sticks

Ice

6 oz. fresh clementine juice

4 oz. gin

Chilled brut Champagne or Prosecco, for topping

PHOTO ON P. 140

This juicy cocktail is a riff on a classic French 75; instead of using lemon juice, F&W's Justin Chapple swaps in clementine juice. For a booze-free version, substitute 4 ounces of apple cider vinegar for the gin and top the cocktails with chilled seltzer instead of Champagne.

1 In a small saucepan, combine sugar, ginger, juniper berries, cranberries, cinnamon sticks, and ½ cup of water and bring to a boil, stirring to dissolve sugar. Remove from heat and let steep for 1 hour. Strain juniper syrup through a fine sieve into a small bowl, pressing on the solids; discard the solids.

2 Fill a cocktail shaker with ice. Add clementine juice, gin, and juniper syrup and shake well. Pour into 8 coupes and top with Champagne. —*Justin Chapple*

Make Ahead
The juniper simple syrup can be refrigerated for up to 2 weeks.

Note
Turn to p. 33 for a classic French 75 recipe.

GOLDEN SPRITZ

— MAKES 1 DRINK —

1¼ oz. Salers

1 oz. Italian bianco vermouth, preferably Contratto

Ice

2 oz. chilled club soda

2 oz. chilled Prosecco

1 lemon twist, for garnish

Salers, a traditional French aperitif made from the bitter root of the gentian plant, has become a pet mixer among US bartenders. Las Vegas bartender Emily Yett adds the yellow liqueur to her crisp vermouth spritz.

In a mixing glass, combine Salers and vermouth. Fill glass with ice and stir well. Strain into a large chilled flute, stir in club soda, and top with Prosecco. Pinch the twist over the drink and add to flute. —*Emily Yett*

ROSIE'S RETURN

— MAKES 1 DRINK —

3 raspberries

¾ oz. London dry gin

¾ oz. Simple Syrup (p. 23)

½ oz. fresh lemon juice

2 drops of orange bitters

1 drop of rosewater

Ice

1½ oz. chilled sparkling rosé

Denver, Colorado, bartender Bryan Dayton likes to serve this pretty pink aperitif before a brunch or dinner celebration. Just one drop of rosewater adds a distinct floral flavor.

In a cocktail shaker, muddle 2 raspberries. Add gin, Simple Syrup, lemon juice, orange bitters, and rosewater. Fill shaker with ice and shake well. Strain into a chilled flute. Top with sparkling rosé and garnish with remaining raspberry skewered on a pick. —*Bryan Dayton*

Rosie's Return

Brunch on the Danube

SONOMA

— MAKES 1 DRINK —

- 2½ oz. chilled unoaked Chardonnay
- ½ oz. Calvados
- 2½ tsp. Honey Syrup (p. 23)
- 1 tsp. verjus
- 2 drops of Salt Solution
- Ice
- 1 lemon twist and 1 thyme sprig, for garnish

PHOTO ON P. 6

L.A. mixologist Devon Tarby uses an unoaked Chardonnay here because it won't overwhelm the other ingredients in the cocktail. To make all the subtle flavors pop, she stirs in a couple of drops of a saltwater solution.

In a mixing glass, combine Chardonnay, Calvados, Honey Syrup, verjus, and Salt Solution. Fill glass with ice, stir well, and strain into a chilled wineglass. Pinch lemon twist over drink and add to glass. Garnish with thyme sprig. —*Devon Tarby*

SALT SOLUTION
Combine 3½ ounces water and 5½ teaspoons kosher salt in a measuring cup and stir until the salt is dissolved. Let stand for 10 minutes. Transfer to a jar and keep at room temperature for up to 1 month. Makes 3½ ounces.

BRUNCH ON THE DANUBE

— MAKES 1 DRINK —

- ¾ oz. Zwack
- ½ oz. tawny port
- ¼ oz. walnut liqueur, such as Nocino della Cristina
- ¼ oz. Simple Syrup (p. 23)
- Ice
- 3 oz. chilled ginger beer
- 1 orange twist, for garnish

Denver, Colorado, bartender Bryan Dayton adds complex herbal flavors to this fizzy aperitif with Zwack, an amaro-like Hungarian liqueur. In the US, many bartenders turn to it as an alternative to Jägermeister. Tawny port is a Portuguese fortified wine often served as an after-dinner drink.

In a mixing glass, combine Zwack, port, walnut liqueur, and Simple Syrup. Fill glass with ice and stir well. Strain into a chilled, ice-filled collins glass, then stir in ginger beer. Pinch orange twist over drink and add to glass. —*Bryan Dayton*

FOUR ON THE FLOOR

MAKES 1 DRINK

- 2 strawberries, 2 raspberries, and 2 blackberries
- 2 lemon twists
- ½ oz. Cinnamon Syrup (p. 23)
- 1 oz. oloroso sherry, preferably Lustau
- 1 oz. East India sherry
- Crushed ice
- 1 mint sprig, for garnish

"This drink is rich and nutty, with ripe fruits that toe the line of winter and spring," says L.A. bartender Karen Grill. "It reminds me of January in Los Angeles."

In a chilled julep cup or rocks glass, muddle 1 of each of the berries with 1 lemon twist and Cinnamon Syrup. Add sherries, then fill cup with crushed ice. Spin a swizzle stick or bar spoon between your hands to mix the drink. Add more crushed ice and garnish with remaining berries skewered on a pick, lemon twist, and mint sprig. —*Karen Grill*

APERITIF

THE DOUBTING DUCK

MAKES 1 DRINK

- 1½ oz. manzanilla sherry
- 1 oz. dry vermouth
- ½ oz. yellow Chartreuse (honeyed herbal liqueur)
- Dash of celery bitters
- Dash of orange bitters
- Ice
- 1 lemon twist skewered on a pick with 1 olive, for garnish

PHOTO ON P. 6

Washington, DC, bartender Derek Brown calls this drink his ideal aperitif because, while it's low-proof, it's also amazingly complex. He loves the manzanilla sherry's savory edge, which makes the drink incredibly food-friendly.

In a mixing glass, combine sherry, vermouth, Chartreuse, and both bitters. Fill glass with ice and stir well. Strain into a chilled coupe and garnish with skewered lemon twist and olive. —*Derek Brown*

Four on the Floor

TANGLED UP

— MAKES 1 DRINK —

2 oz. oloroso or cream sherry

¼ oz. Suze

Ice

4 oz. bitter lemon soda or San Pellegrino Limonata

1 spiral-cut lemon twist, for garnish (p. 20)

"In southern Spain, they love rebujitos," says Washington, DC, bartender Derek Brown about the sherry–lemon soda spritzer. He gives his version a pleasantly bitter boost with Suze, a French aperitif. "It's refreshing," he says, "but you get a little more than just sweet and easy."

In a chilled highball glass, combine sherry and Suze. Fill glass with ice and stir well. Stir in lemon soda and garnish with lemon twist. —*Derek Brown*

HAGAR THE GENTLE

— MAKES 1 DRINK —

1 rosemary sprig

½ oz. Simple Syrup (p. 23)

2 oz. dry vermouth, preferably Dolin

½ oz. Linie aquavit

Dash of absinthe

Ice

4 oz. chilled club soda

1 orange wheel half skewered on a rosemary sprig, for garnish

"I want this drink from about noon till 6 p.m.–bartenders can turn brunch into an all-afternoon affair at the slightest provocation," says New York City bartender Joaquín Simó. "I'd happily have this food-friendly cocktail alongside savory scones, soft scrambled eggs, and piles of shaved jamón."

In a cocktail shaker, muddle rosemary sprig with Simple Syrup. Add vermouth, aquavit, and absinthe; fill with ice and shake well. Fine-strain (p. 20) into a chilled, ice-filled highball glass and stir in club soda. Garnish with skewered orange wheel. —*Joaquín Simó*

Normandie Club Spritz

AMERICANO

MAKES 1 DRINK

1½ oz. Campari

1½ oz. sweet vermouth

3 oz. chilled club soda

Ice

1 orange wheel and 1 lemon twist, for garnish

This drink was a favorite of American expats during Prohibition. Prior to then it was known as the Milano-Torino, for the cities where its two main ingredients were first made: Milan (Campari) and Turin (sweet vermouth).

In a chilled rocks glass, combine Campari, sweet vermouth, and club soda. Fill glass with ice and stir well. Garnish with orange wheel and lemon twist. —*Francesco Lafranconi*

APERITIF

NORMANDIE CLUB SPRITZ

MAKES 1 DRINK

1 oz. dry vermouth, preferably Dolin

1 oz. St-Germain elderflower liqueur

1 oz. fresh grapefruit juice

½ oz. fresh lemon juice

¼ oz. grapefruit liqueur

¼ oz. blanco tequila

¼ oz. pisco, preferably Campo de Encanto

Ice

2½ oz. chilled club soda

1 grapefruit wheel half skewered on a pick, for garnish

Devon Tarby features this lovely, light spritz at The Normandie Club in Los Angeles. "It's like the best grapefruit soda you can imagine," she says, "and tame enough that you can chug a few."

In a cocktail shaker, combine vermouth, St-Germain, grapefruit juice, lemon juice, grapefruit liqueur, tequila, and pisco. Fill shaker with ice and shake for 5 seconds. Strain into a chilled, ice-filled collins glass. Stir in club soda and garnish with grapefruit wheel half. —*Devon Tarby*

BRANDY CRUSTA

— MAKES 1 DRINK —

1 lemon wedge

Sugar

1 long strip of lemon zest

1½ oz. VSOP Cognac

½ oz. orange curaçao

½ oz. fresh lemon juice

¼ oz. maraschino liqueur

2 dashes of Angostura bitters

Ice

This predecessor to the sidecar was invented at the City Exchange bar and café in New Orleans around 1850. NOLA bartender Chris Hannah spikes his modern version with bitters and maraschino liqueur but keeps the sugar rim and signature garnish–a long strip of lemon zest.

Moisten outer rim of a chilled rocks glass with lemon wedge and coat lightly with sugar. Add lemon zest to glass. In a cocktail shaker, combine Cognac, curaçao, lemon juice, maraschino liqueur, and bitters. Fill shaker with ice and shake well. Strain into prepared rocks glass. *—Chris Hannah*

SIDECAR

— MAKES 1 DRINK —

1¾ oz. VSOP Cognac

¾ oz. orange curaçao

¾ oz. fresh lemon juice

¼ oz Simple Syrup (p. 23)

Dash of orange bitters

Ice

1 orange twist, for garnish

According to cocktail expert Dale DeGroff, the sidecar–said to be invented in the 1930s–is an update of a much older drink called the Brandy Crusta (above). While many bartenders consider the sugar rim essential to both drinks, Jonny Raglin asks people their preference. "If no rim, then I simply garnish the drink with a twist."

In a cocktail shaker, combine Cognac, curaçao, lemon juice, Simple Syrup, and bitters. Fill shaker with ice and shake well. Strain into a chilled coupe and garnish with orange twist. *—Jonny Raglin*

VIEUX CARRÉ

MAKES 1 DRINK

1 oz. VSOP Cognac

1 oz. rye whiskey

1 oz. sweet vermouth

1 tsp. Bénédictine (spiced herbal liqueur)

Dash of Peychaud's bitters

Dash of Angostura bitters

Ice

This New Orleans classic, named after the city's French Quarter, was likely created in the 1930s by Walter Bergeron. He tended bar at the establishment that is today called The Carousel Bar.

In a mixing glass, combine Cognac, rye, vermouth, Bénédictine, and both bitters. Fill glass with ice, stir well, and strain into a chilled, ice-filled rocks glass.

CLASSIC

BRANDY ALEXANDER

MAKES 1 DRINK

1½ oz. Cognac

1 oz. white crème de cacao

1 oz. heavy cream

Ice

Pinch of freshly grated nutmeg

Offer this sweet and creamy brandy-based cocktail for a nightcap or dessert. The drink became popular during the early 20th century and is a variation on an earlier gin-based cocktail called an Alexander.

In a cocktail shaker, combine Cognac, crème de cacao, and cream. Fill shaker with ice and shake well. Strain into a chilled martini glass and garnish with nutmeg.

JACK ROSE

— MAKES 1 DRINK —

- **2 oz. bonded apple brandy**
- **¾ oz. fresh lemon juice**
- **¾ oz. grenadine, preferably homemade (p. 23)**
- **Ice**

One theory suggests this drink was named after (and even invented by) Bald Jack Rose, a notorious New York City hit man in the early 20th century. Another theory says the name refers to the applejack (a type of apple brandy) in the recipe and the rose color created by the grenadine.

In a cocktail shaker, combine brandy, lemon juice, and grenadine. Fill shaker with ice and shake well. Strain into a chilled coupe.

FLASHBANG

— MAKES 1 DRINK —

- **2 oz. overproof Cognac, preferably Louis Royer Force 53**
- **½ oz. Branca Menta (bitter, minty Italian digestif)**
- **½ oz. Bénédictine**
- **Ice**

According to Donny Clutterbuck of Cure in Rochester, New York, this drink starts off light, then has a strong finish. "The full effect can be felt after around 10 minutes, and it should take you at least that long to finish it!"

In a cocktail shaker, combine Cognac, Branca Menta, and Bénédictine. Fill shaker with ice and shake well. Strain into a chilled coupe. —*Donny Clutterbuck*

Jack Rose

Frenched Hot Chocolate

FRENCHED HOT CHOCOLATE

12 oz. whole milk

6 oz. yellow Chartreuse (honeyed herbal liqueur)

4 oz. Calvados

2 oz. dark chocolate, chopped

1 vanilla bean, split lengthwise and seeds scraped

One 3-inch cinnamon stick, plus freshly grated or ground cinnamon for garnish

"Chartreuse and chocolate is among the world's most underrated combinations," says Bobby Heugel, co-owner of Anvil Bar & Refuge in Houston. He melds the two ingredients in this boozy, rich hot chocolate.

In a medium saucepan, combine milk, Chartreuse, Calvados, chocolate, vanilla bean and seeds, and cinnamon stick. Stir constantly over moderate heat until chocolate is completely melted. Remove from heat, discard vanilla bean, and whisk hot chocolate until frothy. Ladle into warmed mugs or heatproof glasses and garnish with cinnamon. —*Bobby Heugel*

PCM

1 oz. Peruvian pisco, such as Campo de Encanto

½ oz. fruity red wine, such as Carmenère

¼ oz. buckwheat or other dark honey

Ice

1 lemon twist, for garnish

"There is some rivalry between Peruvian and Chilean pisco distillers, so I wanted to make a cocktail that would bring the two countries together," says Seattle bartender Anu Elford. She combines Peruvian pisco with Chilean Carmenère wine. "In actuality, I might be stirring the pot here. Oh well!"

In a mixing glass, combine pisco, red wine, and honey. Fill glass with ice and stir well. Strain into a chilled coupe. Pinch lemon twist over the drink and add to coupe. —*Anu Elford*

PISCO SOUR

— MAKES 1 DRINK —

2 oz. pisco

¾ oz. fresh lime juice

¾ oz. Simple Syrup (p. 23)

1 large egg white

Ice

4 drops of Angostura bitters, for garnish

The pisco sour is a whiskey sour variation invented in Lima, Peru. Preshaking the drink without ice emulsifies the egg white and gives the drink an airy texture.

In a cocktail shaker, combine pisco, lime juice, Simple Syrup, and egg white and shake vigorously. Fill shaker with ice and shake again. Strain into a chilled coupe. Dot drink with bitters and draw a toothpick through the drops to swirl decoratively.

FROZEN TEA-SCO SOUR

— MAKES 2 DRINKS —

4 oz. Chilean pisco, such as Capel

2 oz. fresh lime juice

2 oz. Matcha Syrup

1½ cups ice cubes

2 strawberries, 2 blueberries, and 2 blackberries skewered on 2 picks, for garnish

New York City bartender Sam Anderson loves this play on a pisco sour: "Green slushy cocktails make me feel like a kid," he says. The matcha syrup and pisco have a cooling effect that makes the drink a terrific match for fiery Mexican-inspired food.

In a blender, combine pisco, lime juice, Matcha Syrup, and ice and blend until smooth. Pour into 2 chilled pilsner or highball glasses and garnish with skewered berries. —*Sam Anderson*

MATCHA SYRUP
In a heatproof jar, combine ¾ teaspoon matcha green-tea powder with 8 ounces hot water. Shake until matcha is dissolved. Add 1 cup sugar and shake until sugar is dissolved. Let cool and refrigerate for up to 2 weeks. Makes about 12 ounces.

Frozen Tea-Sco Sour

Anjou Punch, p. 176

Big Batch

Red Sangria

RED SANGRIA

One 750-ml bottle fruity red
wine, such as Tempranillo or
Garnacha

4 oz. brandy

3 oz. Simple Syrup (p. 23)

1 cup mixed chunks of seeded
oranges, lemons, and limes

Ice

Although Spaniards and Portuguese have been drinking
sangria for centuries, the brandy-spiked drink didn't make
an official appearance in the US until 1964, at the World's
Fair in New York City.

In a pitcher, combine red wine, brandy, Simple Syrup, and fruit.
Refrigerate until chilled and flavors are blended, 4 to 8 hours.
Serve the sangria in chilled, ice-filled wineglasses. —*Bridget Albert*

WHITE SANGRIA

One 750-ml bottle unoaked
white wine, such as
Chardonnay or Vinho Verde

4 oz. brandy

2 oz. Simple Syrup (p. 23)

1 cup mixed chunks of seeded
oranges, lemons, and limes

Ice

Chicago mixologist Bridget Albert usually serves red sangria
at night. She opts for white sangria, which is lighter and
more refreshing, at brunch and daytime parties like showers
and summer barbecues.

In a pitcher, combine white wine, brandy, Simple Syrup and fruit.
Refrigerate until chilled and flavors are blended, 4 to 8 hours.
Serve the sangria in chilled, ice-filled wineglasses. —*Bridget Albert*

EVERYTHING'S COMING UP ROSÉ

MAKES 4 TO 6 DRINKS

8 oz. chilled dry rosé

4 oz. Lillet rosé

4 oz. chilled brewed hibiscus tea

2 oz. fresh lemon juice

2 oz. Simple Syrup (p. 23)

1 oz. Aperol

Ice

4 oz. chilled club soda

Grapefruit wheel halves, lemon wheels, and sliced strawberries, for garnish

Natasha David, co-owner of Nitecap in New York City, creates this sophisticated sangria by combining rosé wine with pleasantly bitter Aperol and delicate, floral hibiscus tea.

In a pitcher or punch bowl, combine rosé, Lillet, tea, lemon juice, Simple Syrup, and Aperol. Fill pitcher with ice and stir well. Stir in club soda and garnish with fruit. Serve in chilled wineglasses.
—*Natasha David*

STAY GOLDEN

MAKES 8 DRINKS

2 black tea bags

16 oz. hot water

2 oz. honey

8 oz. pisco

4 oz. Cocchi Vermouth di Torino

2 oz. yellow Chartreuse (honeyed herbal liqueur)

2 oz. fresh lemon juice

Ice

Lemon wheels and thyme and mint sprigs, for garnish

"In the early days of punch houses," says Chicago bartender Jacyara de Oliveira, "groups would mingle over a bowl and discuss news, politics, and the day-to-day." In keeping with that tradition, she created a pisco-tea punch that's flavorful yet not too strong. "It will get you buzzed, for sure, but allow you to keep up a witty repartee."

1 In a large heatproof measuring cup, steep tea bags in 16 ounces hot water for 4 minutes. Discard tea bags; stir in honey and refrigerate until chilled, about 2 hours.

2 In a pitcher, combine 12 ounces tea with pisco, vermouth, Chartreuse, and lemon juice; add ice and stir well. Pour into chilled rocks glasses and garnish with lemon wheels, thyme, and mint.
—*Jacyara de Oliveira*

Appellation Cooler

PUERTO RICAN RUM PUNCH

MAKES 6 TO 8 DRINKS

5⅓ oz. fresh lime juice

⅓ cup superfine sugar

8 oz. amber rum

2 oz. orange liqueur

2 oz. grenadine

One 750-ml bottle sparkling wine, such as Cava, chilled

Fresh pineapple chunks, for garnish

Many Caribbean cocktails use light rum, but the amber rum here adds sweetness and depth. The punch can easily be doubled and served in a punch bowl if you're having a crowd.

In a large pitcher, combine lime juice and sugar and stir briskly until sugar is dissolved. Add rum, orange liqueur, and grenadine and refrigerate until chilled, about 1 hour. Just before serving, add sparkling wine and pineapple chunks and serve in chilled punch glasses. —*Carolina Buia; Isabel González*

Make Ahead
The rum mixture can be refrigerated overnight. Stir in the sparkling wine and pineapple chunks just before serving.

APPELLATION COOLER

MAKES 4 TO 6 DRINKS

8 oz. dry white wine, preferably Muscadet

4 oz. Cocchi Americano

4 oz. Basil Vermouth

4 tsp. apricot liqueur, preferably Rothman & Winter Orchard Apricot

Ice

4 oz. chilled dry sparkling wine

Seedless cucumber slices, for garnish

"I want to give the white wine spritzer its rightful place in the cocktail world," says New York City bartender Natasha David. She upgrades the oft-diluted, lightweight drink with basil-infused vermouth and Cocchi Americano, a bitter aperitif wine. Her pro tip: "Make sure to eat those punch-soaked cucumber slices!"

In a pitcher, combine wine, Cocchi Americano, Basil Vermouth, and apricot liqueur. Fill pitcher with ice and stir well. Stir in sparkling wine and garnish with cucumber slices. Serve in chilled white wine glasses. —*Natasha David*

BASIL VERMOUTH
In a jar, combine 1 cup loosely packed basil sprigs with 8 ounces Dolin blanc vermouth. Cover and let stand for 1 hour. Strain into another jar and refrigerate for up to 2 weeks. Makes 8 ounces.

CARIBBEAN FAIRY

18 oz. coconut water

6 oz. absinthe

4 oz. sweetened condensed milk

Crushed ice

Freshly grated nutmeg and mint leaves, for garnish

6 young coconut shells, for serving (optional)

"This is seriously the friendliest absinthe drink I've ever had!" says Houston bar impresario Bobby Heugel. "Everyone loves it despite strong opinions on licorice flavors." He serves this creamy but not-too-rich cocktail in young coconut shells and encourages scraping up the coconut flesh with a spoon.

In a pitcher, stir coconut water with absinthe and condensed milk until fully combined. Pour into a punch bowl filled with crushed ice. Garnish with nutmeg. Smack (p. 20) mint leaves over the drink and add to bowl. Ladle into crushed ice–filled coconut shells or chilled, crushed ice–filled rocks glasses. —*Bobby Heugel*

SILK CITY PUNCH

2 Earl Grey tea bags

6 oz. hot water

Crushed ice, plus cubes for serving

6 oz. bourbon

3 oz. amber rum, preferably Ron Zacapa 23

3 oz. Simple Syrup (p. 23)

2 oz. peach liqueur

2 oz. fresh lemon juice

5 lemon wheels, for garnish

The esteemed cocktail historian David Wondrich once told Denver bartender Sean Kenyon that every great punch tastes like delicious iced tea or lemonade. "This one tastes like a refreshing peach tea," Kenyon states.

1 In a large heatproof measuring cup, steep tea bags in hot water for 4 minutes, then discard tea bags. Add crushed ice until brewed tea measures 9 ounces. Let the ice melt and the tea cool completely.

2 In a pitcher, combine tea, bourbon, rum, Simple Syrup, peach liqueur, and lemon juice. Add ice cubes and stir well. Strain into a punch bowl over ice cubes and garnish with lemon wheels. Ladle into chilled punch cups or rocks glasses. —*Sean Kenyon*

PISCO PUNCH

MAKES 12 DRINKS

24 oz. pisco

8 oz. fresh lemon juice
(from about 6 lemons)

8 oz. water

One 8½-oz. bottle pineapple
gum syrup (see Note)

2½ cups fresh pineapple chunks

Ice, preferably 1 large block
(p. 20)

Thin pineapple slices,
for garnish

Ducan Nicol, owner of San Francisco's legendary Bank Exchange bar, invented the pisco punch in the late 1800s. One of the drink's key ingredients, pineapple gum syrup, went out of production long ago and became available again only recently.

In a punch bowl, combine pisco, lemon juice, water, gum syrup, and fresh pineapple chunks and refrigerate until chilled, about 2 hours. Add ice. Serve in chilled coupes and garnish with the pineapple slices. —*Erik Adkins*

Note
Pineapple gum syrup, thickened pineapple-flavored simple syrup, is available at smallhandfoods.com or amazon.com.

Big Batch Tips

Scale your recipe by ratios instead of just multiplying a recipe for a single cocktail by the number of servings you need. In general, you can go with 2 ounces of spirit to ¾ ounce each of citrus and sweetener. You can also think of this as an 8:3:3 ratio.

Batch cocktails in advance and then shake or stir as needed. But if the drink calls for anything with bubbles, combine all the nonbubbly ingredients, keep the mixture as cold as possible, then add the sparkling ingredient at the very end, or as you serve each drink.

ANJOU PUNCH

Three 3-inch cinnamon
sticks, broken into pieces,
plus whole cinnamon sticks
for garnish

8 oz. water

½ cup sugar

Crushed ice

Orange and lemon wheels

12 oz. Cognac

12 oz. Belle de Brillet
(pear liqueur)

9 oz. fresh lemon juice

6 oz. triple sec

12 oz. chilled Champagne

PHOTO ON P. 164

Leo Robitschek of The NoMad Bar in New York City makes
his perfect holiday punch with warming flavors of pear,
cinnamon, and citrus.

1 In a small saucepan, cover the broken cinnamon sticks with the
water and bring to a boil. Simmer over moderately low heat until
reduced by half. Stir in sugar until dissolved. Let cool, then strain
through a fine sieve into a bowl; refrigerate until chilled.

2 Mound crushed ice in the middle of a large punch bowl. Using
a long stirrer or spoon, slide orange and lemon wheels against
the inside of the bowl, then push crushed ice back to keep fruit
in place.

3 In a cocktail shaker, combine one-fourth each of the cinnamon
syrup, Cognac, Belle de Brillet, lemon juice, and triple sec; shake
well. Add one-fourth of the Champagne and shake once, then
add to the punch bowl. Repeat the shaking 3 more times with
the remaining ingredients. Serve the punch in chilled, crushed
ice–filled glasses. Garnish with cinnamon sticks and orange and
lemon wheels. —*Leo Robitschek*

HOMEMADE EGGNOG

—— MAKES 10 DRINKS ——

6 large eggs, separated

¾ cup sugar

24 oz. milk

8 oz. bourbon

4 oz. dark rum

4 oz. brandy

8 oz. heavy cream

½ tsp. freshly grated nutmeg

Salt, for garnish (optional)

Eggnog is usually spiked with brandy, rum, or bourbon. This not-too-rich version includes all three. Salt accents the spirits and helps cut the drink's richness.

1 Put egg yolks in a large bowl and set bowl over a saucepan of simmering water. Add half of the sugar and whisk over low heat until pale yellow and thick, about 5 minutes. Whisk in milk, bourbon, rum, and brandy.

2 In another large bowl, whisk egg whites with remaining sugar until very soft peaks form. Stir whites into yolk mixture. In a medium bowl, beat heavy cream until lightly thickened. Fold whipped cream and nutmeg into eggnog and refrigerate until thoroughly chilled, about 2 hours. Whisk to reblend, then pour into chilled coupes and garnish each drink with a pinch of salt.

ABSINTHE EGGNOG

—— MAKES 4 DRINKS ——

3 large eggs, separated, plus
    1 large egg yolk

¼ cup plus 1 Tbsp. sugar

16 oz. whole milk

4 oz. heavy cream

1½ tsp. pure vanilla extract

¼ tsp. freshly grated cinnamon

⅛ tsp. plus 4 pinches of salt

13 oz. chilled eggnog (above)
    or store-bought eggnog

3 oz. chilled absinthe

Freshly grated nutmeg,
    for garnish

Brooklyn mixologist Maxwell Britten is an absinthe obsessive. Here, he features the anise-flavored spirit in eggnog. For the recipe, Britten prefers a Swiss white absinthe, such as La Clandestine, which tends to be milder than the green varieties.

1 In a large bowl, beat egg whites with a hand mixer until stiff peaks form. Gently fold in ¼ cup sugar. In a medium bowl, beat 4 yolks until combined. Fold yolks into whites, then stir in milk, cream, vanilla, cinnamon, ⅛ teaspoon salt, and remaining 1 tablespoon of sugar. Transfer eggnog to an airtight container and refrigerate until thoroughly chilled, about 2 hours.

2 In a pitcher, combine 13 ounces of eggnog with absinthe and 4 pinches of salt. Stir well and fine-strain (p. 20) into chilled coupes. Garnish each drink with nutmeg. —*Maxwell Britten*

COLONIAL HEIRLOOM

8 oz. chilled brewed
  Earl Grey tea

4 oz. fresh lime juice

  Herbed Oleo-Saccharum

8 oz. London dry gin

8 oz. Batavia-Arrack van
  Oosten (spicy, citrusy
  rum-like spirit)

  Ice

8 oz. chilled club soda

  Lime wheels, rosemary
  sprigs, and kaffir lime
  leaves, for garnish

Houston bartender Bobby Heugel riffs on Bombay Government Punch, a recipe from the early colonial era of India. He adds Earl Grey tea and kaffir lime leaves to his oleo-saccharum–a mix of citrus oil and sugar that many bartenders consider an indispensable ingredient in punches.

1 In a bowl, combine tea and lime juice with oleo-saccharum and stir to dissolve. Strain the liquid into a punch bowl.

2 Add gin and Batavia-Arrack to punch bowl, fill with ice, and stir well. Stir in club soda and garnish with lime wheels, rosemary sprigs, and lime leaves. Serve in chilled punch cups or rocks glasses. —*Bobby Heugel*

HERBED OLEO-SACCHARUM
Using a vegetable peeler, remove zest in strips from 2 lemons and 2 limes, preferably organic. Transfer zests to a shallow medium bowl; add 4 kaffir lime leaves and 2 rosemary sprigs. Add 1 cup sugar and muddle ingredients until zests begin to release their oils. Push zests to sides of bowl, cover, and let macerate overnight. Refrigerate for up to 2 weeks.

Chamomile Lemonade,
p. 183

Mocktails

Mocktails

Nonalcoholic cocktails are making their way onto menus in bars and restaurants across the country, blending delicious combinations of ingredients in refreshing booze-free drinks. These mocktails aren't necessarily meant to taste just like cocktails; rather, they feature quality ingredients in carefully crafted drinks designed to enliven the senses.

STOCKING THE MOCKTAIL BAR

Here are some ingredients you'll need to create memorable nonalcoholic beverages:

Quality Mixers
Higher-quality mixers (both commercial and housemade) such as ginger beer and syrups like grenadine and orgeat give rise to tastier virgin cocktails. (See our recipes for homemade mixers on p. 23.)

Fresh Juice
The fresh juice craze, fueled by blenders and extractors, inspires bright and tasty mocktails. While fresh lemon, lime, orange, and grapefruit juices are always popular, other fresh-squeezed options include apple, grape, kumquat, mango, passion fruit, pineapple, pomegranate, tangerine, and watermelon.

Alternative Sweeteners
Sweeteners ranging from agave to honey and molasses help bartenders prepare better drinks for teetotalers. Other ingredients that can add a hint of sweetness as well as flavor include maple syrup, demerara syrup, turbinado syrup, and sorghum syrup. "Every place in a cocktail should be reserved for a flavor building block. Not just sweet for the sake of sweet," says mixologist Jane Danger. She encourages the use of a broad spectrum of sweeteners in order to craft a well-balanced drink.

Savory Ingredients
Modern mixologists add savory ingredients such as herbs, spices, and teas to their mocktail arsenal to re-create the thrill and complexity of cocktails. Today's mixologists are borrowing from the kitchen—not just techniques, but also ingredients—in order to create innovative drinks. If you're looking to freshen up your mocktails, consider fresh basil, lavender, lemon balm, rosemary, and sage. Spices to keep near the bar include cinnamon, nutmeg, and even cayenne pepper.

BITTERS BUYERS' GUIDE

Bitters are botanical-infused liquids not intended to be consumed on their own, but rather as a flavoring ingredient. Most bitters do contain alcohol, although the alcohol content is negligible and the amount used in a drink is very small (a few drops to $1/8$ teaspoon). While bitters are called for in a number of cocktails, they also add essential flavor and depth to mocktails. Here are a few you may want to keep on hand:

Angostura is one of the most well-known types of aromatic bitters and contains an infused mixture of gentian root, herbs, and spices.

Peychaud's bitters are moderately sweeter than Angostura and slightly fruity with notes of anise and mint.

Orange bitters are made with dried citrus peels and often include hints of coriander and cardamom. Look for Regan's Orange Bitters No. 6 or Fee Brothers.

SALTED LIME RICKEY

—— MAKES 1 DRINK ——

5 pitted Bing cherries

½ lime, cut into wedges

1 Tbsp. sugar

Pinch of salt

Ice

4 oz. chilled club soda

Inspired by Vietnamese-style salted limeade, Ran Duan, owner of The Baldwin Bar outside Boston, revamps a soda fountain throwback. He says the drink is easily adaptable to other fruits, sweeteners, and spices like cardamom and vanilla.

In a cocktail shaker, muddle cherries with lime wedges, sugar, and salt. Fill shaker with ice and shake well. Strain into a chilled, ice-filled highball glass and stir in club soda. —*Ran Duan*

CHAMOMILE LEMONADE

—— MAKES 1 DRINK ——

4 oz. water

2 oz. fresh lemon juice

1½ oz. Chamomile Tea Syrup

Ice

1 lemon wheel and chamomile flowers (optional), for garnish

PHOTO ON P. 180

Devon Tarby, co-owner of the Normandie Club in Los Angeles, is the creator of this not-too-sweet lemonade for grown-ups. She gives the drink a lovely floral flavor with a simple chamomile tea syrup that would also be delicious with club soda.

In a cocktail shaker, combine water, lemon juice, and Chamomile Tea Syrup. Fill shaker with ice and shake well. Strain into a chilled, ice-filled wineglass and garnish with lemon wheel and chamomile flowers. —*Devon Tarby*

CHAMOMILE TEA SYRUP

In a small saucepan, bring 4 ounces water to a boil. Off the heat, steep 2 chamomile tea bags in the water for 5 minutes. Add ½ cup sugar and stir until dissolved. Discard tea bags. Let syrup cool, pour into a jar, and refrigerate for up to 3 weeks. Makes about 5 ounces.

THE SONG DYNASTY

2 oz. chilled club soda

3 oz. fresh grapefruit juice

1 oz. heavy cream

1 oz. Honey Syrup (p. 23)

½ oz. Spicy Ginger Syrup
(p. 23)

½ tsp. matcha green tea powder

Ice

To give this drink a fluffy head of foam, New York City bartender Lacy Hawkins stops straining the ingredients into the glass just below the rim. She then lets the drink rest for 10 seconds before continuing to strain.

Pour club soda into a chilled fizz glass. In a cocktail shaker, combine grapefruit juice, cream, Honey Syrup, Spicy Ginger Syrup, and matcha powder. Fill shaker with ice and shake well. Fine-strain (p.20) into prepared fizz glass. —*Lacy Hawkins*

THAI BASIL, GRAPEFRUIT & CHIA TONIC

32 oz. water

6 oz. fresh grapefruit juice
with pulp

1 oz. pure maple syrup

2 Tbsp. chia seeds

One Thai basil sprig or
4-inch rosemary sprig

Chef Seamus Mullen of New York City's Tertulia restaurant has completely embraced a healthy lifestyle that includes making excellent refreshers like this tonic, which is sweet and tart but also incredibly satisfying, thanks to the chia.

In a large pitcher, combine all ingredients and stir well. Cover and refrigerate for at least 2 hours. Stir before serving. —*Seamus Mullen*

Thai Basil, Grapefruit & Chia Tonic

Hibiscus-Tangerine
Iced Tea

LA ISLA DEL SOL

1 cardamom pod

3 oz. fresh pineapple juice

½ oz. fresh lemon juice

½ oz. Rich Simple Syrup (p. 23)

1 large egg white

3 dashes of aromatic bitters, preferably Fee Brothers

Ice

1 pineapple wedge, for garnish

"This drink is great for times when you're keeping it light but want the fuller flavor of a real cocktail," says Sean Kenyon of Williams & Graham in Denver. (Most bitters are alcohol-based. For a completely nonalcoholic cocktail, leave out the bitters.)

In a cocktail shaker, muddle cardamom pod. Add pineapple juice, lemon juice, Rich Simple Syrup, egg white, and 2 dashes of bitters and shake vigorously. Fill shaker with ice and shake again. Strain into a chilled coupe. Dot with a line of bitters and garnish with pineapple wedge. —*Sean Kenyon*

HIBISCUS-TANGERINE ICED TEA

12 hibiscus tea bags

32 oz. boiling water

16 oz. fresh tangerine juice, plus 1 thinly sliced tangerine

Ice

To cut back on sugar, F&W's Kay Chun mixes sweet tangerine juice with tart hibiscus tea. The result is a very refreshing, fruity drink.

In a heatproof bowl, cover tea bags with boiling water. Let steep for 20 minutes. Strain tea through a fine sieve into another heatproof bowl. Let cool to room temperature, then stir in tangerine juice. Divide tea and all but 4 tangerine slices among 4 ice-filled glasses. Garnish with reserved tangerine slices. —*Kay Chun*

Make Ahead
The tea can be refrigerated for up to 2 days.

CHARLESTON SHRUB

1½ oz. Pineapple Vinegar (p. 122)

1 oz. chilled verjus (see Note)

¾ oz. Honey Syrup (p. 23)

½ oz. fresh lemon juice

Ice

2 oz. chilled club soda

In this supertangy mocktail, New York City mixologist John deBary combines two new additions to the mocktail arsenal: verjus (unripe grape juice) and DIY vinegar. The pineapple vinegar is from Ryan Casey, whose Charleston Sour (p. 120) inspired this recipe.

In a cocktail shaker, combine Pineapple Vinegar, verjus, Honey Syrup, and lemon juice. Fill shaker with ice and shake well. Strain mixture into a chilled, ice-filled highball glass and stir in the club soda. —*John deBary*

Note
Verjus, the tart juice pressed from unripe grapes, is available at specialty food stores.

PHILIPPE KHALLINS

10 oz. Coconut Mix

2 oz. fresh pineapple juice

1 oz. fresh lime juice

Ice

2 kaffir lime leaves and a sprinkle of cayenne pepper, for garnish

New York City bartender Sam Anderson mixes coconut milk with gin and serves the drink in small soup bowls because the flavors are reminiscent of Thai tom kha gai soup. This is his mocktail version.

In a cocktail shaker, combine Coconut Mix, pineapple juice, and lime juice. Fill shaker with ice and shake well. Strain mixture into 2 chilled tea cups and add a few ice cubes. Garnish with lime leaves and cayenne pepper. —*Sam Anderson*

COCONUT MIX
In a saucepan, combine one 13⅔-ounce can unsweetened coconut milk, ⅔ cup sugar, ¼ cup minced fresh ginger, 2 tablespoons sliced fresh lemongrass, 1 small dried Tianjin (Chinese red) chile, and ¼ teaspoon salt. Cook over moderate heat until simmering, 2 to 3 minutes. Remove from heat; add ¼ cup kaffir lime leaves. Let cool, transfer to a jar, and refrigerate overnight. Strain through a cheesecloth-lined sieve into another jar and refrigerate for up to 1 week. Makes about 13 ounces.

Philippe Khallins

Coco Loco

COCO LOCO

1 oz. Coco López sweetened cream of coconut

1 oz. heavy cream

1 oz. fresh pineapple juice

Ice

4 oz. chilled orange soda, such as San Pellegrino Aranciata

Small pinch of freshly grated nutmeg, for garnish

Nashville bartender Ryan Puckett combines his penchant for tiki cocktails with a childhood favorite, orange soda floats; the result is this tropical orange-cream soda. "I'd make orange soda floats with my grandma, so that flavor pairing is something I've always loved," he says.

In a cocktail shaker, combine Coco López, cream, and pineapple juice. Fill shaker with ice and shake well. Pour soda into a chilled, ice-filled collins glass; strain contents of the shaker into glass and garnish with nutmeg. —*Ryan Puckett*

DEEPEST PURPLE, REPRISE

6 Concord grapes

3 shiso leaves

½ oz. Simple Syrup (p. 23)

3 oz. chilled verjus (see Note)

3 ice cubes, plus crushed ice for serving

2 oz. chilled club soda

This mocktail tastes like a sophisticated grape soda; the Japanese herb shiso adds a hit of floral flavor.

In a cocktail shaker, muddle grapes and 2 shiso leaves with Simple Syrup. Add verjus and ice cubes and shake well. Fine-strain (p. 20) into a chilled, crushed ice–filled rocks glass. Stir in club soda and garnish with remaining shiso leaf. —*John deBary*

Note
Verjus, the tart juice pressed from unripe grapes, is available at specialty food stores.

LITTLE PRINCE

5 mint leaves, plus more for garnish

½ oz. Rich Simple Syrup (p. 23)

1¼ oz. fresh lime juice

Ice

6 oz. Club-Mate (available at health clubs and from mateheads.com)

Pinch of finely grated lime zest, for garnish

The base of this crisp mocktail is Club-Mate, a low-sugar energy soda made from yerba mate. The soda, guzzled by German hackers to fuel late-night coding sessions, is gaining cult status in the US.

In a cocktail shaker, combine 5 mint leaves, Rich Simple Syrup, and lime juice. Fill shaker with ice and shake well. Strain into a chilled, ice-filled collins glass and stir in Club-Mate. Garnish with mint leaves and lime zest. —*Maxwell Britten; William Elliott*

WISE GUY

4 sage leaves, plus 1 sprig for garnish

¼ oz. Jalapeño Agave Syrup

1½ oz. fresh pineapple juice

1 oz. verjus (available at specialty food stores)

½ oz. fresh lime juice

Pinch of kosher salt

Ice cubes, plus crushed ice for serving

Pinch of Aleppo pepper, for garnish

"Verjus is an incredible ingredient and is sadly underutilized behind the bar," says bartender Lacy Hawkins. Verjus, the juice of unripened grapes, gives this julep-style mocktail a nuanced tanginess.

In a cocktail shaker, lightly muddle 4 sage leaves with Jalapeño Agave Syrup. Add pineapple juice, verjus, lime juice, and salt. Fill shaker with ice cubes and shake well. Fine-strain (p. 20) into a chilled, crushed ice–filled julep cup and garnish with sage sprig and Aleppo pepper. —*Lacy Hawkins*

JALAPEÑO AGAVE SYRUP

In a heatproof measuring cup, stir 4 ounces agave syrup into 2 ounces hot water until combined. Stir in ½ chopped unseeded jalapeño and let steep for 5 minutes. Strain syrup into a heatproof jar, let cool, and refrigerate for up to 2 weeks. Makes about 5 ounces.

Wise Guy

Meadow Mocktail

MORNING MAI TAI

— MAKES 1 DRINK —

- 1½ oz. chilled apple cider, preferably spiced
- ½ oz. apple cider vinegar
- ½ oz. Ginger Syrup (p. 23)
- ½ oz. fresh lemon juice
- ½ oz. orgeat (almond syrup)
-    Ice cubes, plus crushed ice for serving
- 4 thin red apple slices, for garnish

Apple cider stands in for rum in this alcohol-free version of a mai tai. "The ginger syrup and spiced cider re-create the 'heat' that you experience when drinking spirits," says mixologist John deBary.

In a cocktail shaker, combine apple cider, apple cider vinegar, Ginger Syrup, lemon juice, and orgeat. Fill shaker with ice cubes and shake well. Strain into a chilled, crushed ice–filled double rocks glass, add more crushed ice, and arrange apple slices in a fan on top. —*John deBary*

MEADOW MOCKTAIL

— MAKES 8 DRINKS —

- 1 cup sugar
- 8 oz. water
- ¼ cup dried lavender flowers
- ½ cup basil leaves
- 1 oz. fresh lemon juice
- 11 oz. chilled fresh grapefruit juice
- ¼ oz. Angostura bitters
- 40 oz. chilled sparkling water
-    Ice
-    Basil leaves, grapefruit slices, and/or lavender flowers, for garnish

Johanna Corman of Vena's Fizz House in Portland, Maine, makes this refreshing lavender-and-grapefruit spritzer in large batches for easy summer entertaining.

1 Combine sugar, water, and dried lavender flowers in a medium saucepan and bring to a boil. Cook over moderate heat, stirring, until the sugar dissolves, about 3 minutes. Remove from heat, cover, and let steep for 2 hours. Strain syrup through a fine sieve.

2 In a mini food processor, pulse basil with lemon juice until minced. Scrape into a large pitcher. Stir in 11 ounces lavender syrup (any remaining syrup can be refrigerated for 2 weeks), grapefruit juice, bitters, and sparkling water. Strain into ice-filled glasses and garnish with basil, grapefruit, and lavender. —*Johanna Corman*

Note
For a cocktail version, use 24 ounces sparkling water plus 16 ounces gin or vodka.

EARLY BIRD

2 orange twists

3 oz. cold-brew coffee
concentrate

¾ oz. orgeat (almond syrup)

¼ to ½ oz. Simple Syrup (p. 23)

1 large egg white

Ice

Nashville bartender Ryan Puckett relies on this drink as his morning eye-opener. "It came out of necessity and a mighty hangover," he admits. For the cold-brew coffee, Puckett prefers a nitrogen-infused coffee "that sends you into hyper speed." The recipe here calls for conventional cold-brew coffee concentrate.

In a cocktail shaker, muddle orange twists. Add coffee concentrate, orgeat, Simple Syrup, and egg white and shake vigorously. Fill shaker with ice and shake again. Strain into a chilled coupe. —*Ryan Puckett*

THE SMARTEST BOY ALIVE

2 oz. Fentimans dandelion and
burdock root soda (available
from amazon.com)

1 oz. fresh lemon juice

½ oz. Honey Syrup (p. 23)

5 oz. hot brewed black tea

1 lemon wheel, for garnish

This hot toddy gets depth of flavor from black tea and delicious complexity from Fentimans dandelion and burdock root soda.

In a small saucepan, heat soda, lemon juice, and Honey Syrup over moderate heat until the mixture is hot and soda is flat, 2 to 3 minutes. Stir in tea. Pour into a warmed mug or heatproof glass and garnish with lemon wheel. —*John deBary*

THE THISTLE IN THE PECK

3 basil leaves, plus 1 basil
sprig for garnish

1½ oz. Fennel Syrup (p. 23)

1¾ oz. fresh lime juice

Ice, plus 1 large cube for
serving

This sweet-tart mocktail features fresh lime juice and
a delightfully herbal fennel syrup.

In a cocktail shaker, muddle 3 basil leaves with Fennel Syrup.
Add lime juice, then fill shaker with ice and shake well. Fine-strain
(p. 20) into a chilled rocks glass over the large ice cube and
garnish with basil sprig. —*John deBary*

THE BIRDS & THE BEES

1½ oz. Lemon Verbena Syrup

1 oz. fresh lemon juice

½ oz. Honey Syrup (p. 23)

Ice

4 oz. chilled tonic water

1 lemon balm sprig, for garnish
(optional)

"When I'm making mocktails, flavored syrups are my best
friend," mixologist John deBary says. He sweetens this
refreshing drink with a quick lemon verbena syrup. It has
a lovely citrus-floral flavor that's also fabulous in iced tea.

In a chilled collins glass, combine Lemon Verbena Syrup, lemon
juice, and Honey Syrup. Fill glass with ice and stir well. Stir in
tonic water and garnish with lemon balm. —*John deBary*

LEMON VERBENA SYRUP
In a small saucepan, boil 8 ounces water. Remove from heat
and add ¼ cup dried lemon verbena leaves. Cover and let steep
for 5 minutes. Strain; discard lemon verbena. Stir in ½ cup sugar
until dissolved. Let cool, transfer to a jar, and refrigerate for up
to 3 weeks. Makes about 10 ounces.

BABY MARMALADE

1 oz. chilled verjus (see Note)

1 oz. Ginger Syrup (p. 23)

¾ oz. fresh ginger juice (from a 2-inch piece of grated ginger pressed through a fine strainer)

¾ oz. grenadine, preferably homemade (p. 23)

Ice

1½ oz. chilled club soda

Mixologist John deBary uses both ginger juice and ginger syrup in this spiced mocktail. "Ginger replicates that pleasant burn from the vodka that would typically be used," he says.

In a mixing glass, combine verjus, Ginger Syrup, ginger juice, and grenadine. Fill glass with ice and stir well. Strain into a chilled coupe and stir in club soda. —*John deBary*

Note
Verjus, the tart juice pressed from unripe grapes, is available at specialty food stores.

PSYCHEDELIC BACKYARD

1 lime wedge and coarse salt

1 thin seeded jalapeño slice

One 1-inch-thick banana slice

1½ oz. chilled verjus (see Note above)

1 oz. Raspberry Syrup (p. 23)

¾ oz. fresh lime juice

Ice

To re-create the flavor of banana liqueur, John deBary shakes a chunk of banana into this mocktail. He rims just half the glass with salt so you can choose when to take salty sips.

Moisten half of outer rim of a chilled coupe with lime wedge and coat lightly with salt. In a cocktail shaker, muddle jalapeño. Add banana, verjus, Raspberry Syrup, and lime juice. Fill shaker with ice, shake well, and fine-strain (p. 20) into prepared coupe. —*John deBary*

Psychedelic Backyard

ECTO CHELADA

4 tsp. togarashi (Japanese spice blend of chiles and sesame)

2 tsp. kosher salt

1 lime wedge

24 oz. chilled ginger beer or ginger ale

24 oz. Green Juice Blend

Ice

"I bought a fancy juicer just to make this drink," says bartender Chad Arnholt. "The savory ingredients—cucumbers, peppers, herbs—are unexpected and make the drink feel healthy." He sets out a pitcher of the juice blend for parties, cookouts, or sci-fi movie nights along with tequila, beer, and ginger beer so his guests can customize their own drinks.

1 On a small plate, combine togarashi and salt. Moisten outer rims of 8 chilled collins glasses with lime wedge and coat lightly with spice mix.

2 In each prepared glass, combine 3 ounces ginger beer with 3 ounces Green Juice Blend. Fill each glass with ice and stir well. —*Chad Arnholt*

GREEN JUICE BLEND

In a juicer, juice 1 bunch of mint, 1 bunch of dill, and 1 seeded jalapeño with 3 to 4 green apples to yield 17 ounces of juice. Transfer to a pitcher and add 10 ounces fresh green or yellow tomato juice, 8 ounces fresh cucumber juice, and 2 ounces fresh lime juice. Add 1 teaspoon kosher salt and stir well. Makes about 37 ounces.

CHASING SUMMER

4 oz. Chai Sun Tea

¾ oz. passion fruit puree or juice

½ oz. sweetened condensed milk

¼ oz. balsamic vinegar

Ice cubes, plus crushed ice for serving

"I love this drink so much that it seems like my glass is always empty," says bartender Lacy Hawkins. Her favorite part is the balsamic vinegar. "It adds wonderful acidity to the drink and creates a caramelized finish."

In a cocktail shaker, combine Chai Sun Tea, passion fruit puree, condensed milk, and vinegar. Fill shaker with ice cubes and shake well. Strain into a chilled, crushed ice–filled collins glass.
—*Lacy Hawkins*

CHAI SUN TEA
Place 1 chai tea bag and 12 ounces cold water in a glass jar. Cover and leave in a sunny, warm place for 1 hour. Discard tea bag and refrigerate tea for up to 2 weeks. Makes 12 ounces.

HOT BUTTERED LEMON

2 Tbsp. unsalted butter

2 oz. fresh lemon juice

2 oz. hot water

½ oz. Simple Syrup (p. 23)

1 orange wedge

1 lemon wheel

Pinch of freshly grated nutmeg

Pinch of cinnamon

Melbourne, Australia, bartender Sebastian Reaburn describes this drink as a hot buttered rum crossed with a lemon tart. "The citrus gets softened by the heat and mellowed by the sugar and butter," he says. "It's delicious to nibble on at the end of the drink."

In a small saucepan, melt butter in lemon juice over moderate heat. Add hot water, Simple Syrup, orange wedge, lemon wheel, nutmeg, and cinnamon and cook, stirring, until cloudy and hot. Pour into a small heatproof glass or warmed mug.
—*Sebastian Reaburn*

From left: Madame Ae-Ma,
p. 88; Jalapeño & Rye Whiskey
Chicken Nuggets (top), p. 241;
Charred Shishito Peppers with
Garlic-Herb Oil, p. 219

Bar Food

SPICY LIME LEAF BEER NUTS

1 cup peanut oil, for frying

10 large fresh kaffir lime
leaves (see Note)

8 small dried red chiles

6 cups raw peanuts (2 lbs.)

1 Tbsp. kosher salt

4 large garlic cloves, minced

Andy Ricker, chef and owner of the Pok Pok restaurants in New York and Portland, Oregon, tosses crisp, fried kaffir lime leaves into his spiced nut mix–an example of Thai drinking snacks called kap klaem.

1 In a very large skillet, heat peanut oil. Add lime leaves and chiles and fry over moderate heat until lime leaves are crisp and the chiles turn deep red, about 1 minute. Using a slotted spoon, transfer lime leaves and chiles to paper towels to drain.

2 Add peanuts to skillet and stir-fry over moderate heat until golden brown, about 10 minutes. Using a slotted spoon, transfer peanuts to paper towels to drain. Transfer hot peanuts to a bowl and toss with salt.

3 Add garlic to skillet and fry over moderate heat until golden, about 2 minutes. Using a slotted spoon or fine-mesh skimmer, transfer garlic to paper towels and pat dry.

4 Using your hands, finely crush lime leaves and chiles over peanuts. Add garlic and toss to combine. Transfer peanuts to small bowls and serve warm or at room temperature.
—Andy Ricker

Note
It is important to use fresh (not dried) kaffir lime leaves here. They are available at Asian supermarkets; if sold frozen, defrost before using.

Make Ahead
The peanuts can be stored in an airtight container for up to 1 week.

MAPLE-GLAZED PEANUTS & BACON

3 thick slices of bacon (3 oz.)

1 Tbsp. thyme leaves, minced

1 Tbsp. kosher salt

¾ tsp. Old Bay Seasoning

½ tsp. cayenne pepper

½ tsp. dry mustard

3 cups unsalted roasted peanuts (1 lb.)

½ cup pure maple syrup

Sweet, salty, and a little spicy, these beer nuts are from chef Meg Grace Larcom, the culinary director at the Kitchen Bistros and Hedge Row in Denver.

1 Preheat oven to 325°. In a medium skillet, cook bacon over moderate heat until crisp, about 6 minutes. Transfer bacon to paper towels to drain, then finely chop.

2 In a medium bowl, mix thyme, salt, Old Bay, cayenne, and dry mustard. Add peanuts, maple syrup, and bacon and toss until peanuts are evenly coated. Scrape nuts onto a parchment paper–lined baking sheet and roast for about 30 minutes, stirring once, until maple syrup has thickened. Let peanuts cool completely, stirring frequently to break up any large clumps. Serve in glass jars or a large bowl. —*Meg Grace Larcom*

Make Ahead
The peanuts can be stored in an airtight container for up to 5 days.

Petty Cash Guacamole

PETTY CASH GUACAMOLE

—— MAKES ABOUT 2 CUPS ——

- 2 small ripe Hass avocados— peeled, pitted, and cut into large chunks
- 2 Tbsp. fresh lime juice
- 2 Tbsp. finely chopped cilantro
- 1 Tbsp. roasted pepitas, chopped
- 1 Tbsp. chopped tomato
- ½ serrano chile, minced
- 1 tsp. finely chopped red onion
- Kosher salt
- Tortilla chips, for serving

The salty crunch of pepitas (hulled pumpkin seeds) makes this creamy, spicy guacamole from L.A.'s Petty Cash taqueria especially good.

In a blender, puree avocados and lime juice until smooth. Transfer puree to a small bowl and stir in cilantro, pepitas, tomato, chile, and onion. Season with salt and serve with tortilla chips. —*Walter Manzke*

TRUFFLED POPCORN

—— MAKES 6 SERVINGS ——

- 6 Tbsp. unsalted butter
- 1 Tbsp. minced black truffle (optional, see Note.)
- 1 tsp. white truffle oil
- Salt
- 3 Tbsp. vegetable oil
- 1 cup popcorn kernels
- Freshly ground pepper

Upgrade plain popcorn to a fancy bar snack by adding minced black truffle and white truffle oil.

1 In a small saucepan, melt butter over low heat. Stir in truffle, truffle oil, and a pinch of salt; keep warm.

2 In a large, heavy pot, heat vegetable oil. Add popcorn kernels, cover, and cook over moderate heat until they start popping. Cook, shaking pot continuously, until popping has almost stopped. Carefully pour popcorn into a very large bowl. Add truffled butter and toss well. Season with salt and pepper and serve at once. —*F&W*

Note
Jarred truffle shavings are available at specialty food stores.

ENDLESS CARAMEL CORN

MAKES 20 CUPS

3 Tbsp. vegetable oil, plus more for greasing

½ cup popcorn kernels

1½ tsp. baking soda

1 tsp. adobo sauce (from a can of chipotle chiles in adobo)

3 cups sugar

3 Tbsp. unsalted butter

1 Tbsp. kosher salt

½ cup water

Salty, sweet, and amazingly crisp, this caramel-coated popcorn gets a hit of spice from the adobo sauce in canned chipotle chiles.

1 Lightly coat a large bowl and 2 large rimmed baking sheets with oil. In a large saucepan, combine 3 tablespoons oil and popping corn. Cover and cook over moderate heat until corn starts to pop. Shake pan and cook until corn stops popping, about 5 minutes. Transfer popcorn to prepared bowl.

2 In a small bowl, whisk baking soda with adobo sauce. In a large saucepan, combine sugar with butter, salt, and ½ cup water and bring to a boil, stirring until sugar dissolves. Boil mixture over moderate heat without stirring until a golden caramel forms, about 13 minutes. Remove from heat and stir in adobo mixture; the syrup will foam. Immediately drizzle hot caramel over popcorn and, using 2 greased spoons, toss to coat. Spread caramel corn on prepared baking sheets in an even layer and let cool completely before serving. —*Stephen Jones*

Make Ahead
The caramel corn can be stored in an airtight container for up to 5 days.

PIMENTO CHEESE

MAKES 6 SERVINGS

3 red bell peppers

5 oz. sharp yellow cheddar cheese, coarsely shredded (2 cups)

4 oz. cream cheese (½ cup), softened

¼ cup mayonnaise

1 Tbsp. juice from a jar of bread-and-butter pickles (optional)

¼ tsp. Tabasco

Kosher salt

Freshly ground pepper

Saltine crackers, for serving

Atlanta chef Linton Hopkins became a pimento cheese convert when he tried his wife's recipe. "The sharpness of the cheddar cuts through the mayo so you get a more dynamic flavor," he says. Hopkins insists on roasting his own peppers, and then mixing in the charred bits.

1 Roast peppers directly over a gas flame or under a preheated broiler, turning, until charred all over. Transfer peppers to a bowl, cover with plastic wrap, and let steam for 15 minutes. Peel, seed, and stem roasted peppers, then cut into ⅛-inch dice; pat dry with paper towels.

2 In a medium bowl, mix diced peppers with cheddar, cream cheese, mayonnaise, pickle juice, and Tabasco and season with salt and pepper. Cover and refrigerate for at least 2 hours. Serve with crackers. —*Linton Hopkins*

CREAMY, CHEESY ARTICHOKE DIP

MAKES 8 SERVINGS

2 Tbsp. extra-virgin olive oil

1 large shallot, minced

2 garlic cloves, minced

One 9-oz. package frozen artichoke hearts, thawed and drained

¼ cup dry white wine

8 oz. cream cheese, softened

1 cup shredded Gruyère cheese

2 Tbsp. finely chopped parsley

1½ Tbsp. fresh lemon juice

1 tsp. Tabasco

½ cup plus 2 Tbsp. freshly grated Parmigiano-Reggiano cheese

Kosher salt

Freshly ground pepper

¼ cup panko

New York City chef Michael White's version of the classic cheesy, warm dip makes great use of frozen artichokes: They're simmered with garlic and wine; mixed with cream cheese, Gruyère, and Tabasco; and baked with a panko breadcrumb topping.

1 Preheat oven to 400°. In a skillet, heat oil. Add shallot and garlic and cook over moderate heat, stirring, until softened, about 3 minutes. Add artichoke hearts and cook, stirring, until heated through, about 5 minutes. Add wine and simmer until most of the liquid has evaporated, about 3 minutes; let cool.

2 In a bowl, combine cream cheese, Gruyère, parsley, lemon juice, Tabasco, and ½ cup Parmigiano. Fold in artichoke mixture and season with salt and pepper. Scrape into a shallow 3-cup baking dish and sprinkle panko and remaining Parmigiano on top. Bake for about 20 minutes, until heated through and lightly golden on top. Serve with toast points and crudités. —*Michael White*

CHICKPEA FRITTERS WITH SALSA VERDE

Salsa Verde

1½ Tbsp. minced shallot

¾ tsp. kosher salt, divided

1½ Tbsp. tomato or apple cider vinegar

1½ cups parsley leaves

1½ cups basil leaves

½ cup olive oil

½ small garlic clove

½ tsp. ground piment d'Espelette

Chickpea Fritters

6 Tbsp. olive oil

2 garlic cloves

2½ cups water

1½ cups chickpea flour

1 Tbsp. kosher salt, divided

4 cups neutral oil (such as canola), for frying

Chef Lachlan Mackinnon-Patterson pairs these addictive little chickpea-flour morsels (called panelle in Sicily, where they're a popular street snack) with pickled shallot–flecked salsa verde, making them the perfect post-work nosh.

1 Make the salsa verde: In a small bowl, sprinkle minced shallot with ½ teaspoon salt. Add vinegar, and let stand at least 20 minutes.

2 Process herbs, ½ cup olive oil, garlic, and piment d'Espelette in a blender on high speed to reach a pesto-like consistency. (Do not overblend or sauce will turn brown.) Transfer salsa verde to an airtight container and refrigerate until ready to serve.

3 Make the chickpea fritters: Puree 6 tablespoons olive oil and garlic cloves in a blender until smooth. Pour through a fine wire-mesh strainer into a small bowl, pressing gently on solids. Discard solids.

4 Bring 2½ cups water to a boil in a medium pot, covered, over high heat. Whisk in chickpea flour and 1½ teaspoons salt until smooth. Fold in oil mixture with a heatproof spatula. Reduce heat to moderately low and cook, stirring often with spatula to ensure mixture does not stick to sides or bottom of pot, 15 minutes. Remove from heat and let cool slightly. Transfer mixture to a food processor and process until smooth.

5 Place chickpea mixture in a 9-by-13-inch pan lined with plastic wrap. Top with another layer of plastic wrap and press mixture to fill pan. Mixture should be about ¼ inch thick. Refrigerate until set, about 30 minutes.

6 Heat neutral oil in a large saucepan or small Dutch oven to 350°. Break chickpea mixture into roughly 1-inch squares. Fry in 3 or 4 batches, agitating gently with a mesh skimmer or large slotted spoon to ensure even frying, until crispy and slightly golden, 3 minutes. Drain on paper towels. Sprinkle with remaining 1½ teaspoons salt.

7 Drain shallots and add to salsa verde. Season with remaining ¼ teaspoon salt and stir to combine. Serve fritters with salsa verde. —*Lachlan Mackinnon-Patterson*

Buffalo Fried Pickles

BACON-WRAPPED CHERRY PEPPERS

MAKES 4 TO 6 SERVINGS

6 jarred hot cherry peppers—
halved through the
stem, seeded, drained,
and patted dry

⅓ cup cream cheese, softened

12 thin bacon slices (6 oz.)

These super-easy hors d'oeuvres from Bluestem in Kansas City, Missouri, are a spicy, cheesy riff on traditional devils on horseback (bacon-wrapped dates). They're perfect for parties because they can be prepped ahead of time.

1 Preheat oven to 350°. Stuff each cherry pepper half with a heaping teaspoon of cream cheese and wrap with a slice of bacon; secure with a toothpick.

2 Arrange peppers in a large ovenproof skillet and cook over moderate heat, turning, until bacon is browned, 12 to 15 minutes. Transfer skillet to oven; bake for 5 minutes, until bacon is crisp and cream cheese is hot. Serve warm. —*Colby Garrelts*

BUFFALO FRIED PICKLES

MAKES 4 SERVINGS

Vegetable oil, for frying

2 kosher dill pickles (about
6 inches long), sliced
lengthwise ¼ inch thick

All-purpose flour, for
dredging

2 large eggs beaten with
2 Tbsp. water

1 cup fine dry breadcrumbs
mixed with 1 tsp. cayenne
pepper

Blue cheese salad dressing
and hot sauce, for serving

According to chef David Bull of Second Bar + Kitchen in Austin, Texas, these popular bar snacks have just the right ratio of breading to pickle. "Plus, we serve them with a pretty intense Gorgonzola dip, which doesn't hurt either," he says.

1 In a large saucepan, heat 1½ inches oil to 375°. Pat pickle slices dry with paper towels. Put flour, eggs, and breadcrumbs in 3 separate shallow bowls. Dredge pickle slices in flour, shaking off the excess. Dip them in egg, then coat with breadcrumbs.

2 Fry pickles, about 5 slices at a time, turning once, until browned and crisp, about 1 minute. Transfer to paper towels to drain. Serve hot, with blue cheese dressing and hot sauce. —*David Bull*

FRIED OKRA WITH JALAPEÑO JELLY

— MAKES 4 TO 6 SERVINGS —

2 cups buttermilk

3 garlic cloves, smashed

½ tsp. Tabasco

Kosher salt

1 cup all-purpose flour

1 cup fine stone-ground cornmeal

½ tsp. cayenne pepper

½ tsp. freshly ground black pepper

1 lb. okra, stemmed (see Note)

Canola oil, for frying

Jalapeño pepper jelly, for serving

Punch Bowl Social's chef Sergio Romero, who is from Mississippi, loves serving fried dishes with sweet-spicy pepper jelly. Be sure to use fine cornmeal and tender okra.

1 In a medium saucepan, combine buttermilk, garlic, Tabasco, and 1 tablespoon of salt and bring to a simmer. Remove from heat and let steep for 10 minutes. Using a slotted spoon, remove garlic, and discard. Let buttermilk cool completely.

2 Set a rack over a baking sheet. In a large bowl, whisk flour with cornmeal, cayenne, black pepper, and 1½ teaspoons of salt. Dip okra in buttermilk, letting the excess drip back into pan, then dredge in cornmeal mixture. Transfer coated okra to rack.

3 In a large saucepan, heat 1½ inches of canola oil to 350°. Working in batches, fry okra until golden, about 4 minutes. Using a slotted spoon, transfer okra to paper towels to drain; sprinkle with salt. Serve right away, with jalapeño pepper jelly.
—*Sergio Romero*

Note
Cut off the stems just at the base, leaving the pods intact, to avoid producing okra's characteristic slime.

CHARRED SHISHITO PEPPERS WITH GARLIC–HERB OIL

Garlic-Herb Oil

- 3 cups grapeseed oil
- 1 bunch of parsley (about 4 cups loosely packed)
- 1 bunch of cilantro (about 4 cups loosely packed)
- 10 basil leaves
- 10 mint leaves
- 4 garlic cloves
- 2 tsp. grated lime zest
- 2 tsp. Champagne vinegar
- 1 tsp. kosher salt
- ⅛ tsp. cayenne pepper
- 1 tsp. fresh lime juice

Shishito Peppers

- 1 lb. shishito peppers
- 2 Tbsp. neutral oil (such as grapeseed or canola)
- 1 tsp. kosher salt
- 1 Tbsp. fresh lime juice
- 1 tsp. flaked sea salt (such as Maldon)
- 1 tsp. grated lime zest

PHOTO ON P. 204

At his sleek Houston bar, chef Justin Yu pairs blistered shishito peppers with bright green, zesty garlic-herb oil, a take on persillade. You'll want to keep this stuff around–it's fantastic drizzled on salads or tossed with hot pasta.

1 Make the garlic-herb oil: Set a large heatproof bowl in an ice bath. In a large saucepan, heat 3 cups grapeseed oil over moderate heat until shimmering. Add parsley, cilantro, basil, mint, and garlic and fry, stirring, until the herbs are bright green and fragrant, about 15 seconds. Working carefully and quickly, pour oil mixture into a blender. Begin blending on low, gradually increasing speed to high until the herbs are completely incorporated, about 2 minutes.

2 Pour the garlic-herb oil into the prepared bowl and fold until the mixture is chilled, about 1 minute. Add 2 teaspoons lime zest, Champagne vinegar, kosher salt, and cayenne and stir to combine. Chill until ready to serve.

3 Make the shishito peppers: Heat a 12-inch cast-iron skillet over high heat. Toss the peppers with 2 tablespoons oil and kosher salt. Add half of the peppers to the pan; cover and cook the peppers until charred, about 8 minutes.

4 Uncover the peppers and toss until just cooked through, about 10 seconds. Place cooked peppers in a bowl. Repeat procedure with remaining peppers. Dress warm peppers with 1 tablespoon lime juice and flaked salt.

5 To serve, season the garlic-herb oil with 1 teaspoon lime juice and transfer to a large shallow bowl set on a large serving platter. Arrange shishito peppers around the bowl for dipping, and sprinkle the peppers with 1 teaspoon lime zest and serve.
—*Justin Yu*

SMOKED TROUT DEVILED EGGS

MAKES 8 SERVINGS

8 large hard-boiled eggs, peeled and halved lengthwise

4 oz. skinless smoked-trout fillet, flaked

¼ cup mayonnaise

1 Tbsp. chopped parsley

½ tsp. curry powder

Kosher salt

Freshly ground pepper

1 Tbsp. chopped salted roasted almonds

The deviled eggs at New York City's Pegu Club are as stellar as the expertly made cocktails. It's the hickory-smoked trout and curry mayonnaise in the filling that elevate this cocktail party standby.

Scoop yolks from 12 hard-boiled egg halves into a bowl. (Reserve remaining yolks for another use.) Add trout, mayonnaise, parsley, and curry powder; season with salt and pepper. Mix well to break up trout. Mound filling in egg whites and arrange on a platter. Garnish with almonds and serve. —*Gavin Citron*

DANGER TOTS

MAKES 6 SERVINGS

Vegetable oil, for frying

One 32-oz. package frozen Tater Tots

Kosher salt

1½ cups shredded sharp cheddar cheese

½ cup prepared guacamole

¼ cup sour cream

3 slices of bacon, cooked until crisp and crumbled

1 plum tomato—halved, seeded, and cut into ¼-inch dice

1 jalapeño, thinly sliced

Loaded with cheddar, bacon, sour cream, and guacamole, these amped-up Tater Tots aren't on the menu at PDT in Manhattan, but insiders know to ask for them.

1 In a large, deep skillet, heat 1 inch of vegetable oil to 400°. Working in batches, fry Tater Tots, stirring once or twice, until golden and crisp, about 3 minutes. Transfer to paper towels to drain and season with salt.

2 Preheat broiler. Pile fried Tater Tots on an ovenproof serving plate and sprinkle with cheese. Broil 2 inches from heat for about 1 minute, or until cheese is melted. Spoon guacamole and sour cream over Tater Tots, sprinkle with bacon, tomato, and jalapeño and serve. —*Jane Danger*

POMMES FRITES

2 lbs. baking potatoes, peeled and cut into ¼-inch-thick sticks

Vegetable oil, for frying

4 garlic cloves, crushed

1 Tbsp. finely chopped rosemary

Kosher salt

Dijon mustard, for serving

Jonathon Sawyer's twice-fried pommes frites are legendary at The Greenhouse Tavern in Cleveland. Now they're also served at Sawyer's Street Frites at First Energy football stadium. The menu there includes the classic garlic-rosemary recipe here as well as carbonara, salt-and-vinegar, and mozzarella-and-gravy frites.

1 In a medium bowl, cover potatoes with water and let stand for 15 minutes. Drain, then rinse potatoes and pat thoroughly dry.

2 In a large saucepan, heat 2 inches vegetable oil to 275°. Line a baking sheet with paper towels. Working in batches, fry potatoes until almost tender and slightly translucent, about 5 minutes. Transfer the potatoes to paper towels to drain. Refrigerate for 30 minutes.

3 Reheat oil to 350°. In a mortar, pound garlic with rosemary and a pinch of salt until a paste forms. Fry potatoes in batches until golden and crisp, about 5 minutes. Using a slotted spoon, transfer fries to a large rimmed baking sheet and immediately season with salt. Toss with garlic-rosemary paste and serve right away, with Dijon mustard alongside. —*Jonathon Sawyer*

MINTY PEAS & BACON ON TOAST

— MAKES 4 SERVINGS —

1 cup frozen peas, thawed

2 Tbsp. unsalted butter, softened

2 Tbsp. cream cheese, softened

¼ cup lightly packed mint leaves, plus chopped mint for garnish

Kosher salt

Cayenne pepper

Four ½-inch-thick slices of sourdough bread

Extra-virgin olive oil, preferably fruity, for brushing and garnish

12 thin bacon slices (6 oz.)

Chef Greg Vernick is a toast expert: He serves several kinds as appetizers at Vernick Food & Drink in Philadelphia. Here, he purees frozen peas with mint and butter to spread on thick slices of sourdough bread with bacon on top. The toasts soak up the bacon fat in the oven.

1 Preheat oven to 400°. In a food processor, combine peas with butter, cream cheese, and ¼ cup mint. Pulse until nearly smooth; season pea butter with salt and cayenne.

2 Brush bread with olive oil and arrange slices on a rimmed baking sheet. Toast bread in oven for about 8 minutes, turning once, until lightly golden but still chewy in the center. Transfer toasts to a work surface; leave oven on.

3 Spread each piece of toast with about ¼ cup pea butter and top with 3 slices of bacon. Arrange toasts on baking sheet and bake for about 10 minutes, until bacon just starts to render. Turn on broiler and broil the toasts 6 inches from the heat for about 3 minutes, until bacon starts to brown. Garnish toasts with olive oil and chopped mint and serve warm. —*Greg Vernick*

NACHOS WITH PINTO BEANS & JACK CHEESE

1 lb. tomatoes

1 white onion, halved lengthwise

3 garlic cloves

2 chipotles in adobo sauce, stemmed

1½ cups water

Kosher salt

Freshly ground pepper

3 poblano chiles

One 1-lb. bag tortilla chips

1 lb. Monterey Jack cheese, shredded

One 15-oz. can pinto beans, rinsed and drained

Mexican crema or sour cream, guacamole, cilantro, and minced white onion, for serving

"Nachos are my dirty little secret snack," says San Francisco chef Traci Des Jardins. "They can be so delicious if you use great sturdy chips, freshly roasted chiles, and a good salsa."

1 Light a grill or preheat a grill pan. Grill tomatoes, halved onion, and garlic over moderately high heat, turning, until charred in spots, about 10 minutes. In a saucepan, simmer tomatoes, onion, garlic, and chipotles with 1½ cups of water over moderate heat until onion is softened and tomatoes burst, about 30 minutes. Transfer to a blender and puree until smooth. Season with salt and pepper.

2 Roast poblanos over a gas flame, turning, until charred. Transfer to a bowl, cover with plastic, and let steam for 15 minutes. Peel, seed, and stem chiles, then dice them.

3 Preheat oven to 425°. Layer half of chips on a foil-lined rimmed baking sheet. Scatter half of cheese, beans, and diced poblanos over chips. Repeat layering with remaining chips, cheese, beans, and poblanos. Drizzle half of the salsa on top and bake for about 10 minutes, until cheese is melted. Drizzle crema over nachos, top with guacamole and remaining salsa, then sprinkle with cilantro and minced onion. Serve immediately. —*Traci Des Jardins*

FOUR-CHEESE GRILLED PESTO PIZZA

½ cup unsalted roasted pistachios

2 small garlic cloves

2 cups lightly packed baby arugula

1 cup lightly packed basil leaves

½ tsp. crushed red pepper

½ cup extra-virgin olive oil, plus more for brushing

½ cup freshly grated Parmigiano-Reggiano cheese

Kosher salt

Freshly ground black pepper

½ cup each of shredded mozzarella, Fontina, provolone, and scamorza cheeses

1 lb. pizza dough

This crowd-pleasing white pizza is lightly charred on the grill and topped with a garlicky pistachio pesto and four cheeses: mozzarella, Fontina, provolone, and scamorza (a cow-milk cheese that's like a dry mozzarella). If scamorza isn't available, double the amount of mozzarella.

1 In a food processor, pulse pistachios and garlic until minced. Add arugula, basil, and crushed red pepper and pulse until minced. With machine on, gradually add ½ cup oil until incorporated. Add Parmigiano and pulse to combine. Season pesto with salt and black pepper.

2 Light a grill or preheat a grill pan. In a bowl, toss mozzarella with Fontina, provolone, and scamorza.

3 Divide dough into 4 pieces. On a lightly floured work surface, roll or stretch each dough piece to a 10-inch oval, ⅛ inch thick. Brush dough with oil. Grill each pizza over moderately high heat, turning once, until lightly charred on both sides and puffed, about 4 minutes. Transfer dough to a work surface. Spread one-fourth of the pesto on top of dough and sprinkle with cheeses. Season with salt and pepper.

4 Working in batches if necessary, grill pizzas over moderately low heat, covered, until cheese is just melted, about 5 minutes. Cut pizzas into strips and serve hot. —*Matt Troost*

NEW SHRIMP COCKTAIL

1 gallon water

1 lemon, cut into 8 wedges, plus more for garnish

1 bay leaf

1 tsp. black peppercorns

½ tsp. Old Bay Seasoning

Kosher salt

18 jumbo shrimp, shelled and deveined

1 cup ketchup

¼ cup peeled, seeded, and minced cucumber

1 Tbsp. minced red onion

1 Tbsp. finely grated peeled fresh horseradish (or jarred horseradish), plus more for garnish

1 Tbsp. fresh lemon juice

1 tsp. finely grated lemon zest

1 serrano chile, seeded and minced

1 tsp. Worcestershire sauce

¼ tsp. Tabasco

Freshly ground pepper

This reimagined shrimp cocktail from Boston chef Stefan Jarausch features a vibrant horseradish cocktail sauce that includes big chunks of chopped shrimp. He reserves a few jumbo shrimp for dipping into the sauce.

1 In a large saucepan, combine 1 gallon of water with 8 lemon wedges, bay leaf, peppercorns, Old Bay, and 1 teaspoon of salt and bring to a boil. Add shrimp and return to a boil. Remove from heat, cover, and let shrimp poach until just opaque throughout, about 5 minutes. Drain and rinse shrimp with cold water, then refrigerate until chilled, 30 minutes.

2 In a medium bowl, mix all remaining ingredients and season with salt and pepper. Cut 12 shrimp into 1-inch pieces and fold them in. To serve, spoon chopped shrimp salad into 6 glasses or bowls and top with remaining whole shrimp. Garnish with freshly grated horseradish and lemon wedges. —*Stefan Jarausch*

SHRIMP GYOZA

¼ cup plus 1 Tbsp. vegetable oil

4 oz. shiitake mushrooms, stems discarded and caps thinly sliced

4 oz. asparagus, thinly sliced crosswise

1 medium shallot, sliced

1 lb. shelled and deveined shrimp

4 Tbsp. oyster sauce

2 Tbsp. chopped cilantro

1 scallion, finely chopped

½ tsp. kosher salt

One 10- to 12-oz. package gyoza wrappers

Honolulu restaurant Lucky Belly offers these juicy dumplings with a citrus-soy dipping sauce and edamame-avocado puree. But the shrimp-and-shiitake-stuffed gyoza are delicious on their own.

1 In a skillet, heat 1 tablespoon oil. Add shiitake, asparagus, and shallot and stir-fry over high heat until softened, about 8 minutes. Transfer to a bowl to cool. In a food processor, pulse half of the shrimp until smooth. Coarsely chop remaining shrimp. Add all of the shrimp to asparagus mixture along with oyster sauce, cilantro, scallion, and salt.

2 Working in batches, lightly brush edges of gyoza wrappers with water. Spoon a scant tablespoon of filling in the center of each wrapper and fold wrapper in half, pressing to seal. Arrange gyoza on a wax paper–lined baking sheet, seam side up, and cover with a damp paper towel.

3 Divide remaining ¼ cup oil between 2 large nonstick skillets. Arrange gyoza in skillets seam side up in 2 concentric circles without touching. Cook over high heat until bottoms are lightly browned, about 2 minutes. Add ½ cup water to each skillet, cover and cook until water has evaporated and dumplings are cooked through, about 5 minutes. Uncover skillets and cook until gyoza bottoms are browned and crisp, about 1 minute. Transfer the gyoza to a plate and serve. —*Jesse Cruz*

OYSTERS ON THE HALF SHELL WITH CEVICHE TOPPING

1 tsp. coriander seeds

¼ cup finely diced peeled Asian pear

¼ cup peeled, seeded, and finely diced cucumber

1 serrano chile, seeded and minced

1 Tbsp. minced cilantro

1 Tbsp. fresh lime juice

1 tsp. minced candied ginger

1 tsp. Asian fish sauce

1 tsp. extra-virgin olive oil

Kosher salt

Freshly ground pepper

12 freshly shucked oysters on the half shell, such as Rappahannocks

Virginia chef Dylan Fultineer is always dreaming up new ways to show off Chesapeake Bay oysters, and this is one of his favorites. The combination of raw seafood and a tangy cilantro-chile topping evokes ceviche.

1 In a small skillet, toast coriander seeds over moderate heat until fragrant, about 2 minutes. Let cool, then coarsely crush seeds in a mortar. In a small bowl, mix crushed coriander with all remaining ingredients except oysters.

2 Arrange oysters on crushed ice. Spoon some of the topping on each one and serve right away, passing additional topping at the table. —*Dylan Fultineer*

CHUNKY CRAB CAKES

AIOLI

- 1 roasted red bell pepper—peeled, seeded, and stemmed
- 1 cup mayonnaise
- 1 garlic clove
- 1 Tbsp. fresh lemon juice
- Kosher salt
- Freshly ground pepper

CRAB CAKES

- ½ cup mayonnaise
- 1 large egg, lightly beaten
- 2 Tbsp. minced red onion
- 2 Tbsp. minced red bell pepper
- 1½ Tbsp. fresh lemon juice
- 1 Tbsp. minced jalapeño
- 2 tsp. Dijon mustard
- 2 tsp. Worcestershire sauce
- 1 tsp. hot sauce
- 1 lb. jumbo lump crabmeat
- ¾ cup panko, plus more for dredging
- ½ cup vegetable oil

Chef Bernie Kantak originally made these crab cakes for a special cocktail pairing dinner at Citizen Public House in Scottsdale, Arizona. They were so popular that the restaurant added them to the regular menu.

1 Make the aioli: In a food processor, puree roasted red pepper, mayonnaise, garlic, and lemon juice. Season with salt and pepper and scrape into a small bowl.

2 Make the crab cakes: In a large bowl, combine all ingredients except crab, panko, and oil; mix well. Gently fold in crab and ¾ cup panko. Scoop into ten 1-inch-thick patties, dredge in panko and transfer to a plate.

3 In a large skillet, heat ¼ cup oil. Fry half of crab cakes over moderate heat until golden and cooked through, about 3 minutes per side. Transfer to paper towels to drain. Wipe out skillet and repeat with remaining oil and crab cakes. Serve with aioli.
—*Bernie Kantak*

TUNA TARTARE CRISPS

- 32 thin baguette slices, cut from a medium loaf
- ¼ cup mayonnaise
- 1 tsp. wasabi paste
- Kosher salt
- Freshly ground pepper
- ½ pound sushi-grade tuna, cut into ¼-inch dice
- 3 Tbsp. soy sauce
- 1 Hass avocado, cut into ¼-inch dice
- ⅓ cup finely diced seedless cucumber
- 1 scallion, thinly sliced
- 2 tsp. chopped pickled ginger

PHOTO ON P. 250

A hybrid of tuna tartare and tuna-avocado sushi rolls, these crisps from chef Lee Hefter get an extra punch of flavor from pickled ginger and wasabi mayo. Here, the tartare is served on baguette toasts, but you can also spoon it on potato chips.

1 Preheat oven to 350°. Toast baguette slices on a large baking sheet until light golden and crisp, about 15 minutes. Let cool.

2 In a small bowl, mix mayonnaise with wasabi paste and season with salt and pepper.

3 In a medium bowl, gently mix tuna with soy sauce, avocado, cucumber, scallion, and ginger. Spoon a dollop of the wasabi mayonnaise onto each toast, top with tuna tartare, and serve.
—Lee Hefter

CHICKEN CRISPS

MAKES 4 SERVINGS

½ cup vegetable oil

5 garlic cloves, very thinly sliced

¾ lb. chicken skin in large pieces (from 3 to 4 chickens), excess fat removed

Kosher salt

Togarashi (Japanese seasoning mix)

Whole-grain mustard, for brushing

Honey, for drizzling

Finely grated lime zest, for garnish

Crispy chicken skins rival fried pork rinds. Chef Matthias Merges bakes them until crackly, then tops them with sweet and salty seasonings.

1 Preheat oven to 375° and line 2 baking sheets with parchment paper. In a small saucepan, combine vegetable oil with sliced garlic and cook over moderate heat, stirring often, until garlic is golden and crisp, about 8 minutes. Using a slotted spoon, transfer garlic chips to paper towels to drain.

2 Spread out chicken skin in a single layer on the prepared baking sheets and season lightly with salt and togarashi. Top chicken skin with another sheet of parchment paper and another baking sheet to weigh it down. Bake for 40 to 50 minutes, until skins are golden and crisp; rotate baking sheets from front to back and top to bottom halfway through baking.

3 Transfer crispy chicken skins to paper towels to drain. Lightly brush with whole-grain mustard and transfer to a serving bowl. Drizzle lightly with honey, garnish with garlic chips and lime zest, and serve. —*Matthias Merges*

Make Ahead

The crispy chicken skins and garlic chips can be kept at room temperature for up to 3 hours. Brush with mustard and drizzle with honey before serving.

CHICKEN & POBLANO TACOS WITH CREMA

— MAKES 4 SERVINGS —

5 poblano chiles

4 boneless chicken thighs with skin (1 lb.), pounded ½ inch thick

Extra-virgin olive oil, for brushing

Kosher salt

Freshly ground pepper

½ cup chopped cilantro

12 warm corn tortillas

Mexican crema or sour cream, shredded romaine lettuce, chopped white onion, and lime wedges, for serving

To make these tacos extraordinary, chef Justin Large recommends roasting the poblanos over an open flame until they're charred and blistered all over. "Roasting the chiles adds an unbelievable depth and presence to the dish."

1 Roast poblanos directly over a gas flame or under a preheated broiler, turning, until charred all over. Transfer chiles to a bowl, cover with plastic wrap, and let steam for 15 minutes. Peel, seed, and stem chiles, then cut them into ¼-inch strips.

2 Light a grill or preheat a grill pan. Brush chicken all over with oil and season with salt and pepper. Grill over moderately high heat, turning once, until skin is crisp and browned, about 8 minutes. Transfer chicken to a carving board and cut into ½-inch strips.

3 In a medium bowl, toss poblano strips with chicken and cilantro and season with salt and pepper. Serve chicken-poblano filling in warm tortillas with crema, lettuce, onion, and lime wedges. —*Justin Large*

CHIPOTLE CHICKEN TACOS

MAKES 4 SERVINGS

- 8 **bone-in chicken thighs (3 lbs.)**
- 2 **Tbsp. vegetable oil, plus more for brushing**
- **Kosher salt**
- **Freshly ground pepper**
- ½ **medium white onion, minced, plus more for serving**
- 2 **jalapeños—stemmed, seeded, and minced**
- 2 **Tbsp. minced chipotle chiles plus 3 Tbsp. adobo sauce from the can or jar**
- 4 **plum tomatoes, finely chopped**
- **Warm corn tortillas, cilantro leaves, sour cream, and lime wedges, for serving**

PHOTO ON P. 252

Alex Stupak is the chef and owner of Manhattan's Empellón Taqueria and co-author of *Tacos: Recipes and Provocations.* For this recipe, he roasts and shreds juicy chicken thighs, then tosses the meat in a smoky tomato sauce kicked up with chipotle chiles.

1 Preheat oven to 350°. On a large rimmed baking sheet, brush chicken with vegetable oil and season with salt and pepper. Bake for about 45 minutes, until an instant-read thermometer inserted in largest piece registers 165°. Let cool, then shred meat; discard skin and bones.

2 In a large skillet, heat 2 tablespoons vegetable oil until shimmering. Add ½ onion, jalapeños, and a generous pinch of salt and cook over moderate heat, stirring occasionally, until just softened, about 5 minutes. Add chipotles and adobo sauce and cook for 2 minutes. Add tomatoes and cook until they have softened and any liquid has evaporated, about 7 minutes. Stir in shredded chicken and cook until hot, about 3 minutes. Season with salt and pepper.

3 Spoon chicken into warm corn tortillas and serve with cilantro, sour cream, lime wedges, and minced onion. —*Alex Stupak*

CAMBODIAN RED CURRY CHICKEN WINGS

3 Tbsp. canola oil, divided

2 lbs. chicken wings, tips discarded

2 shallots, minced

4 garlic cloves, minced

2 lemongrass stalks, tender white inner bulbs only, finely chopped

2 Tbsp. minced fresh ginger

2 small dried chiles de árbol, stems discarded

2 Tbsp. soy sauce

1 Tbsp. Asian fish sauce

1 tsp. ground cumin

1 tsp. ground coriander

½ tsp. paprika

½ tsp. freshly grated nutmeg

½ tsp. ground turmeric

1 cup unsweetened coconut milk

Kosher salt

Lime wedges, for serving

Boldly flavored and nicely spiced, these Cambodia-inspired wings from chef Edward Lee of 610 Magnolia and Milkwood in Louisville, Kentucky, require a pile of napkins for wiping the delicious red curry coconut sauce off your fingers. For a heartier meal, serve the wings over rice.

1 In a large skillet, heat 2 tablespoons oil. Working in 2 batches, cook wings over moderate heat, turning, until golden all over. Transfer to a paper towel–lined plate to drain.

2 Add remaining 1 tablespoon oil to skillet along with shallots, garlic, lemongrass, and ginger; cook over low heat, stirring, until softened, 3 minutes. Stir in chiles, soy sauce, fish sauce, cumin, coriander, paprika, nutmeg, and turmeric and cook until fragrant, 3 minutes. Stir in coconut milk. Transfer mixture to a blender and puree sauce.

3 Return sauce to skillet. Add chicken and toss to coat. Cover and cook over low heat until cooked through, 10 minutes. Uncover and cook, stirring, until sauce is thick, 5 minutes. Season with salt and serve with lime wedges. —*Edward Lee*

IKE'S VIETNAMESE FISH SAUCE WINGS

MAKES 6 SERVINGS

½ cup Asian fish sauce

½ cup superfine sugar

4 garlic cloves—2 crushed, 2 minced

3 lbs. chicken wings, split at the drumettes

2 Tbsp. vegetable oil, plus more for frying

1 cup cornstarch

1 Tbsp. chopped cilantro

1 Tbsp. chopped mint

Customers wait for hours for these incredible wings at the Pok Pok locations in Portland, Oregon, and New York City. In the summer, the Portland restaurant goes through 3,500 pounds of wings a week. They're chef-owner Andy Ricker's re-creation of a popular drinking snack that he discovered at a Saigon bia hoi ("fresh beer") stand in 2001.

1 In a large bowl, whisk fish sauce, sugar, and crushed garlic. Add wings and toss to coat. Refrigerate for 3 hours, tossing wings occasionally.

2 In a small skillet, heat 2 tablespoons oil. Add minced garlic and cook over moderate heat until golden, about 3 minutes. Drain on paper towels.

3 In a large pot, heat 2 inches oil to 350°. Pat wings dry on paper towels; reserve marinade. Spread cornstarch in a shallow bowl, add wings and turn to coat. Fry wings in batches until golden and cooked through, about 10 minutes per batch. Drain on paper towels and transfer to a serving bowl.

4 In a small saucepan, simmer marinade over moderately high heat until syrupy, about 5 minutes. Strain sauce over wings and toss. Top with cilantro, mint, and fried garlic and serve.
—Andy Ricker

JALAPEÑO & RYE WHISKEY CHICKEN NUGGETS

MAKES 32 NUGGETS

NUGGETS

- 2 lbs. skinless, boneless chicken thighs, diced
- 8 tsp. kosher salt, divided
- 2 Tbsp. rye whiskey, divided
- 2 large egg whites, beaten
- ¼ cup minced shallot
- 3 garlic cloves, minced
- 2 jalapeños, minced
- 4 cups all-purpose flour, divided
- 2 tsp. freshly ground black pepper
- 4 cups buttermilk, divided
- 6 cups neutral oil, for frying
- ⅜ tsp. baking soda
- ⅜ tsp. baking powder
- Fine sea salt, for seasoning

DIPPING SAUCE

- ½ cup honey
- ¼ cup Dijon mustard
- ¼ cup whole-grain mustard

PHOTO ON P. 204

To make these crispy bites, chef Zoe Schor employs the French technique for making mousseline. Double-breaded and fried, these are the ultimate homemade chicken nuggets—juicy and insanely crisp.

1 Make the nuggets: In a food processor, pulse chicken, 4 teaspoons kosher salt, and 1 tablespoon whiskey until smooth. With machine running, add egg whites. Scrape mixture into a bowl and fold in shallot, garlic, and jalapeños.

2 Divide mixture into 32 (1-ounce) balls; flatten into nuggets on a parchment paper–lined baking sheet. Freeze until solid, about 3 hours.

3 In a 7-by-11-inch baking dish, whisk together 2⅔ cups flour, remaining 4 teaspoons kosher salt, and pepper. Place 1⅓ cups buttermilk in a second 7-by-11-inch baking dish. Working carefully in batches, dredge nuggets in seasoned flour, then dip in buttermilk, then flour again, trying not to incorporate excess buttermilk into flour. Place breaded nuggets on a wire rack. Reserve seasoned flour.

4 In a large heavy pot, heat oil to 325°. Working in batches, fry nuggets until golden brown, about 4 minutes. Transfer to a paper towel–lined tray and let cool completely. Reserve oil.

5 Heat frying oil to 350°. Sift seasoned flour to remove any clumps. Measure sifted flour and add fresh flour as needed to equal 1⅓ cups. Whisk together seasoned flour and remaining 2⅔ cups buttermilk until smooth; add remaining 1 tablespoon whiskey, baking soda, and baking powder, and whisk to combine. Working in 4 batches of 8, dredge the cooled nuggets in batter, allowing excess to drip back into bowl. Carefully lower nuggets into oil and fry, gently turning and stirring with a mesh skimmer, until golden brown, 3 to 4 minutes. Remove from oil, season immediately with fine sea salt, and transfer to a paper towel–lined tray.

6 Make the dipping sauce: Stir honey and mustards together; serve with nuggets. —*Zoe Schor*

CARNITAS & CHUTNEY GRILLED CHEESE SANDWICH

CARNITAS

- 2 lbs. boneless pork shoulder
- 2 tsp. kosher salt
- 1 tsp. freshly ground black pepper
- 1 Tbsp. neutral oil (such as canola)
- 1 orange, halved
- 1 cup whole milk
- 5 thyme sprigs
- 1 bay leaf

SANDWICH

- 1 oz. Verde Capra blue cheese or other blue cheese, crumbled
- 1 oz. aged white cheddar cheese, shredded
- ½ oz. Parmesan cheese, grated
- 1 Tbsp. minced parsley
- 1 tsp. finely minced shallot
- 1 Tbsp. mayonnaise
- 1 tsp. whole-grain mustard
- 2 artisan organic sourdough bread slices, lightly toasted
- 3 Tbsp. store-bought spiced apple chutney or preserves
- 2 Tbsp. unsalted butter

Three types of cheese, tender pork, and tart spiced apple chutney make up this delicious grilled sandwich from Santa Monica, California, chef Raphael Lunetta. The carnitas recipe makes enough shredded pork for 12 sandwiches, though you may find other delicious uses for it. If you like, substitute leftover pulled pork for the carnitas for a quick sandwich fix.

1 Make the carnitas: Preheat oven to 275°. Season pork shoulder with salt and pepper. Heat oil in a large Dutch oven over moderate heat. Sear pork shoulder until golden brown all over, 5 to 6 minutes per side. Remove pork from pan. Pour off drippings and discard. Return pork to pan and squeeze juice from orange halves over pork. Add spent orange rinds to pan along with milk, thyme sprigs, and bay leaf. Cover with a lid or 2 layers of aluminum foil and roast in oven until very tender, pork is sizzling in fat, and a meat thermometer registers 195°, 3 to 4 hours. Let pork rest for 20 minutes. Shred pork, discarding any large pieces of fat.

2 Make the sandwich: In a small bowl, fold together blue cheese, cheddar, Parmesan, parsley, and shallot. In a second small bowl, stir together mayonnaise and mustard.

3 Spread each slice of bread with the mayonnaise-mustard mixture. Top 1 slice with cheese mixture, ⅓ cup carnitas, and chutney, then top with remaining bread slice.

4 Melt butter in a cast-iron skillet or griddle over moderate heat. Add the sandwich and top with another skillet or heavy heatproof plate. Cook until bread is golden and cheese is melted, about 5 minutes per side and serve. —Raphael Lunetta

From top left: 22 Punch, p. 144;
Chickpea Fritters with Salsa Verde, p. 215;
Carnitas & Chutney Grilled Cheese Sandwiches

KOGI DOGS

2 cups finely shredded cabbage

1 large scallion, finely chopped

1 Tbsp. fresh lime juice

Kosher salt

Freshly ground pepper

½ cup mayonnaise

1 Tbsp. toasted sesame seeds, crushed

1 Tbsp. vegetable oil, plus more for brushing

1 cup kimchi, drained and patted dry

8 hot dog buns

8 all-beef hot dogs, partially split

1 cup shredded sharp cheddar cheese

2 cups shredded romaine lettuce

1 small onion, thinly sliced

2 cups cilantro sprigs

Sriracha, for drizzling

Bacon-wrapped "dirty dogs" have been a longtime staple for late-night diners in Los Angeles. Chef Roy Choi, king of the Kogi food truck empire, thought it was time for an upgrade. "I wanted to dress mine to the nines with our best toppings: Napa cabbage salad, kimchi, and toasted-sesame mayo," he says. "Make sure to crisp out the hot dogs so there's a nice snap when you bite into them," he adds.

1 In a large bowl, toss cabbage with scallion and lime juice; season with salt and pepper. In a small bowl, mix mayonnaise with sesame seeds and season with salt.

2 In a medium nonstick skillet, heat 1 tablespoon of oil. Add kimchi and cook over high heat until browned, about 3 minutes.

3 Light a grill or preheat a grill pan. Brush cut sides of hot dog buns with oil and grill over moderately high heat until toasted on both sides, about 45 seconds total. Spread cut sides of buns with sesame mayonnaise.

4 Grill hot dogs over moderately high heat until nicely charred all over. Tuck them in buns; top with kimchi, cheddar, cabbage salad, lettuce, onion, and cilantro. Drizzle with Sriracha and serve. —*Roy Choi*

LOLA BURGERS

MAKES 4 SERVINGS

8 **thick-cut slices of smoky bacon (½ lb.)**

1½ **lbs. mixed ground sirloin and chuck**

Kosher salt

Freshly ground pepper

4 **slices of smoked cheddar cheese (2 oz.)**

4 **large eggs**

4 **English muffins, toasted**

¼ **cup pickled cocktail onions, thinly sliced**

Ketchup and mustard, for serving

This mash-up of a hamburger and breakfast sandwich is from chef Michael Symon, whose Cleveland-area restaurant empire includes the B Spot burger chain. He piles a beef patty, smoked cheddar, bacon, and an oozy fried egg on a toasted English muffin.

1 In a large nonstick skillet, cook bacon over moderate heat until crisp, about 6 minutes. Drain on paper towels. Pour off all but 1 tablespoon of bacon fat in skillet.

2 Preheat a grill pan. Shape meat into four 5-inch patties and season generously with salt and pepper. Grill over moderately high heat until lightly charred, about 3 minutes. Flip burgers and top with smoked cheddar. Cook for about 3 minutes longer for medium-rare meat.

3 Meanwhile, in reserved bacon fat in skillet, fry eggs over-easy over moderate heat, about 3 minutes. Set burgers on bottoms of English muffins and top with pickled onions, bacon, and fried eggs. Close burgers and serve with ketchup and mustard.
—*Michael Symon*

BLUE SMOKE BLACK PEPPER RIBS

MAKES 8 SERVINGS

2 Tbsp. coarsely ground pepper

2 Tbsp. brown sugar

1 Tbsp. kosher salt

1 tsp. pimentón de la Vera

2 racks pork baby back ribs (about 4½ lbs.)

Inspired by barbecue joints in Texas, the peppery beef ribs served at Blue Smoke in Manhattan are replete with hickory smoke. The cheater's version here calls for easier-to-find pork ribs and pimentón de la Vera, smoked Spanish paprika.

1 Preheat oven to 350°. In a small bowl, mix pepper with sugar, salt, and smoked paprika. Sprinkle both sides of ribs with pepper mixture. Place ribs meaty side up on a large rimmed baking sheet and bake for 2½ hours, or until the meat begins to pull away from the bones.

2 Transfer ribs to a cutting board and let stand for 5 minutes. Cut racks into individual ribs and serve. —*Blue Smoke*

POLPETTE IN SPICY TOMATO SAUCE

MAKES 12 SERVINGS

1 lb. ground veal

½ lb. sweet Italian sausage, casings removed

1 cup dry breadcrumbs

½ cup whole milk

3 garlic cloves, minced

2 Tbsp. chopped parsley

2 large egg whites

1 Tbsp. tomato paste

½ cup freshly grated Pecorino Romano cheese, plus more for sprinkling

Salt and black pepper

2½ cups prepared tomato sauce

Pinch of crushed red pepper

Ruggero Gadaldi serves these hearty veal-and-sausage meatballs at Beretta, his Italian comfort-food restaurant in San Francisco. They were inspired by the bold red-sauce cuisine on *The Sopranos*, one of Gadaldi's favorite TV shows.

1 Preheat oven to 350°. In a large bowl, mix veal with sausage, breadcrumbs, milk, garlic, parsley, egg whites, tomato paste, and ½ cup pecorino; season with salt and black pepper. Roll into 1½-inch meatballs. Bake meatballs on a lightly oiled baking sheet for about 30 minutes, until browned and cooked through.

2 In a saucepan, season tomato sauce with crushed red pepper. Add meatballs and simmer until sauce is slightly thickened, about 8 minutes. Sprinkle with pecorino and serve. —*Ruggero Gadaldi*

Blue Smoke Black Pepper Ribs

Guides + Menus

Madame Ae-Ma, p. 88

PARTY APPETIZER MENUS

Looking to pair a creative cocktail with just the right snack? Check out these 24 menu ideas for your next holiday gathering or special occasion.

New Year's Day Open House

Everything's Coming Up Rosé, p. 168

Tuna Tartare Crisps, p. 233

Valentine's Day Dinner

Martini, p. 32

Oysters on the Half Shell with Ceviche Topping, p. 231

Oscar Night Gala

Golden Spritz, p. 146

Truffled Popcorn, p. 211

Mardis Gras Parade

French 75, p. 33

Pommes Frites, p. 221

St. Patrick's Day Party

Irish Coffee, p. 133

Minty Peas & Bacon on Toast, p. 222

Easter Brunch

Tropical Mimosa, p. 143

Smoked Trout Deviled Eggs, p. 220

Tuna Tartare Crisps, p. 233; Cosmopolitan, p. 98

Minty Peas & Bacon, p. 222; Skyliner, p. 100

From left: Spicy Lime Leaf
Beer Nuts, p. 206; Normandie
Club Spritz, p. 155

Chipotle Chicken Tacos, p. 237

Blue Smoke Black Pepper Ribs, p. 246; Old-Fashioned, p. 118

Carnitas & Chutney Grilled
Cheese Sandwich, p. 242;
22 Punch, p. 144

Shrimp Gyoza, p. 229

COCKTAIL STYLE GUIDE

Use this guide to find just the kind of drink you are in the mood for—be it a light and airy before-dinner drink, a fizzy refresher, a classic highball, or a relaxing nightcap. Categories include preparation method (shaken, stirred, or built in the glass), texture, style, or occasion. If you're looking for a nonalcoholic beverage, turn to the Mocktails chapter (p. 180) for a collection of refreshing booze-free drinks.

Norseman, p. 48

Coco Cooler, p. 111

La Picosa, p. 80

PDT/Crif Frozen Piña
Colada, p. 70

Normandie Club Spritz,
p. 155

Matcha Milk Punch,
p. 112

CONVERSION CHART

In Cocktails, measures for spirits and other liquids are given in fluid ounces.
Use the chart below if you need to convert to cup measures.

CUP		OUNCE		TBSP	TSP
1 cup	=	8 fl oz.			
¾ cup	=	6 fl oz.			
⅔ cup	=	5⅓ fl oz.			
		5 fl oz.	=	10 Tbsp.	
½ cup	=	4 fl oz.			
		3 fl oz.	=	6 Tbsp.	
⅓ cup	=	2⅔ fl oz.			
¼ cup	=	2 fl oz.			
		1 fl oz.	=	2 Tbsp.	
		½ fl oz.	=	1 Tbsp.	3 tsp.
		⅓ fl oz.	=	⅔ Tbsp.	2 tsp.
		¼ fl oz.	=	½ Tbsp.	1½ tsp.

1 oz. = about 32 dashes
1 dash = 4 to 5 drops

Mai Tai, p. 54

COCKTAIL INDEX

Page numbers in **bold** indicate photographs.

Tingling Negroni, p. 30

Rosa Armago, p. 93

T

V

BAR FOOD INDEX

A

Artichoke Dip, Creamy, Cheesy, 214

ASPARAGUS

Shrimp Gyoza, 229

AVOCADOS

Petty Cash Guacamole, **210,** 211

Tuna Tartare Crisps, 233

B

BACON

Bacon-Wrapped Cherry Peppers, 217

Danger Tots, 220

Lola Burgers, 245

Maple-Glazed Peanuts & Bacon, **208,** 209

Minty Peas & Bacon on Toast, 222, **223, 250**

Beans & Jack Cheese, Nachos with Pinto, **224,** 225

BEEF

Burgers, Lola, 245

Kogi Dogs, 244

Buffalo Fried Pickles, **216,** 217

Burgers, Lola, 245

C

Caramel Corn, Endless, 212, **213**

Carnitas & Chutney Grilled Cheese Sandwich, 242, **243, 253**

Ceviche Topping, Oysters on the Half Shell with, **230,** 231

CHEESE

Carnitas & Chutney Grilled Cheese Sandwich, 242, **243, 253**

Creamy, Cheesy Artichoke Dip, 214

Danger Tots, 220

Four-Cheese Grilled Pesto Pizza, 226, **227**

Kogi Dogs, 244

Lola Burgers, 245

Nachos with Pinto Beans & Jack Cheese, **224,** 225

Pimento Cheese, 214

Polpette in Spicy Tomato Sauce, 246

CHICKEN

Cambodian Red Curry Chicken Wings, 238, **239**

Chicken Crisps, **234,** 235

Chicken & Poblano Tacos with Crema, 236

Chipotle Chicken Tacos, 237

Ike's Vietnamese Fish Sauce Wings, 240

Jalapeño & Rye Whiskey Chicken Nuggets, **204,** 241

Chickpea Fritters with Salsa Verde, 215, **243**

CHILES

Chicken & Poblano Tacos with Crema, 236

Chipotle Chicken Tacos, 237

Fried Okra with Jalapeño Jelly, 218

Jalapeño & Rye Whiskey Chicken Nuggets, **204,** 241

Nachos with Pinto Beans & Jack Cheese, **224,** 225

Spicy Lime Leaf Beer Nuts, 206, **207**

Crab Cakes, Chunky, 232

Crema, Chicken & Poblano Tacos with, 236

D

DIPS & SPREADS

Creamy, Cheesy Artichoke Dip, 214

Petty Cash Guacamole, **210,** 211

Pimento Cheese, 214

DUMPLINGS

Shrimp Gyoza, 229

E

EGGS

Lola Burgers, 245

Smoked Trout Deviled Eggs, 220

F

FISH. See also Shellfish

Smoked Trout Deviled Eggs, 220

Tuna Tartare Crisps, 233

Fish Sauce Wings, Ike's Vietnamese, 240

Fritters with Salsa Verde, Chickpea, 215, **243**

G

GARLIC

Cambodian Red Curry Chicken Wings, 238, **239**

Charred Shishito Peppers with Garlic-Herb Oil, **204,** 219

Chicken Crisps, **234,** 235

Ike's Vietnamese Fish Sauce Wings, 240

Pommes Frites, 221

Spicy Lime Leaf Beer Nuts, 206, **207**

Guacamole, Petty Cash, **210,** 211

Bacon-Wrapped Cherry
Peppers, p. 217

PDT/Crif Frozen Piña Colada, p. 70

PHOTO CREDITS

Golden Spritz, p. 146

More books from
FOOD & WINE

Perfect Pairings

With chapters arranged by the most popular grape varieties, this collection of classic recipes takes the guesswork out of which dish to serve with your favorite wines. The easy-to-follow wine primers explain the nuances of the grapes and regions so you can shop for bottles like a pro.

Master Recipes

This must-have manual breaks down the best way to DIY everything from beef jerky to babka. With step-by-step instructions and photos, star chefs like Jacques Pépin and David Chang share their foolproof methods for over 180 delicious dishes. Along the way, you'll learn indispensable skills like fermenting pickles, making bread, and tempering chocolate.

Mad Genius Tips

Did you know that you can poach a dozen eggs in a muffin tin? Or grate ginger with a fork? Or ripen bananas in the oven? Discover clever shortcuts and unexpected uses for everyday tools in a book that's as helpful as it is entertaining. Justin Chapple, the star of FOOD & WINE's Mad Genius Tips video series, shares more than 90 hacks for 100+ easy, fun, and delicious recipes.